SELECTING A LOCAL AREA NETWORK

Richard G. Lefkon

AMA Management Briefing

AMA MEMBERSHIP PUBLICATIONS DIVISION
AMERICAN MANAGEMENT ASSOCIATION

Library of Congress Cataloging-in-Publication Data

Lefkon, Richard G.
  Selecting a local area network.

  (AMA management briefing)
  1. Computers—Purchasing. 2. Local area networks (Computer networks)—Purchasing.
  I. Title. II. Series.
  HD9696.C62L445 1986   004.6'8'029   86-22152
  ISBN 0-8144-2328-0

©1986 Membership Publications Division

American Management Association, New York.

This Management Briefing has been distributed to all members enrolled in the General and Administrative Services and Information Systems Technology divisions of the American Management Association. Copies may be purchased at the following single-copy rates: AMA members, $17.95. Nonmembers, $19.95.

First Printing

Contents

To **Hinda** and **Irving**, who first
showed me how to establish
and maintain networks.

How to Use this Book

In the near future, any company that owns a mainframe or many PCs will at least consider acquiring one or more LANs. This book introduces all of the basic concepts of LANs, and it follows up each concept in enough depth for the reader to negotiate intelligently when the time comes to budget for and implement the right LAN for that location.

Those who know a great deal about LANs will obtain full value from this book if they start and end with the Appendix, the Network Evaluation Form for LAN Selection. As long as these readers find one or two questions to put to their suppliers (questions they wouldn't have asked had they not worked through the form), this publication will have achieved its purpose.

Those who start with the Appendix but desire a context for some of the questions can turn to the corresponding section of Chapter Thirteen. That chapter summarizes the other sections of the book, but casts the material in the same topic sequences as the Network Evaluation Form.

Chapters Two through Twelve examine the various technical aspects in some depth. These can be referenced, selectively skipped, or read "cover to cover," depending on the reader's interests, corporate needs, and level of expertise in each topic.

Chapter One presents the basic terminology of LANs. An understanding of this vocabulary (especially that of the OSI layers) is frequently assumed in the other chapters.

Some tables in the book list competing products for certain aspects of LANs. These tables should not be taken as complete listings of all that is available. Also, although representatives from most of the best-known vendors have authored chapters pertaining to their specialties, the selection offered here should be considered a *starting point,* rather than a limitation on the suppliers to be considered.

The data processing or office automation manager who is just starting out in LANs and who anticipates a limited number of network workstations may wish to reference the chapters individually. In this case, the advice of a retail dealer of proven reliability can be extremely valuable.

Companies with some experience in LANs—or companies anticipating a large eventual budget for data communications—will want to learn enough to negotiate directly with the primary LAN suppliers. In this case, all (or nearly all) of the specialized chapters should be read before filling out the selection form in the Appendix. For very large existing or anticipated networks, it may be worth the cost in staff time to interview or visit other installations, or to do a trial implementation onsite.

Note: Material from various vendors contained herein is provided for informational purposes only, and does not imply an endorsement on the part of the American Management Association or the author.

1

Introduction to Local Area Networks

Nearly half a century ago, the earliest computers could fill a room with their tubes and electromechanical switches. But by the end of the 1970s, the typical large office had several word processing machines, and American families were graduating from video games to home computers.

When two or more computers are linked together so they can communicate, the whole arrangement can be termed a *network*. A telephone company is a good example of a network, even though most of the devices it weaves together have no computer intelligence.

This book concerns networks that are local in two senses: confined physically to lines within a single factory, office building, or campus complex; and controlled completely by the owner, not some regulatory agency. If it satisfies both these requirements, a network may be called a local area network (LAN). The telephone company, on the other hand, is sometimes referred to as a *wide* area network (WAN).

There is one more requirement for a truly local area network: Each device, regardless of size or sophistication, must start with an equal ability to access all other devices. The earliest computer networks did not have this equal "connectivity," and all their joined devices had to communicate through the central mainframe computer rather than talk directly to one another.

The LAN concept has grown increasingly popular within the past decade. First implemented for small office equipment, then for personal computers, LANs are now being applied to robots.

LANs permit an organization to expand by one workstation at a time instead of adding another large computer. Another benefit is that a LAN can "distribute" the processing, either sharing printers and other resources, or spreading the workload among several workstations at the same time.

CONNECTIVITY, SHAPE, AND ADAPTABILITY

Of the three basic network shapes ("topologies") shown in Figure 1.1, the star shape is most familiar to users of large mainframe or minicomputers, such as IBM, Honeywell, Burroughs, Digital, Hewlett Packard, Control Data, and Data General. It also applies to voice or data private branch exchanges (PBXs), such as Rolm or Micom, and even to some networks of personal computers in which all the outlying stations are physically connected to communication ports on a particular PC at the center. LANs *de*centralize processing. Star networks with hubs that do a lot more than forward each signal without modification are not true local area networks because they lack equal connectivity among stations.

Figure 1.1 Star, ring, and bus.

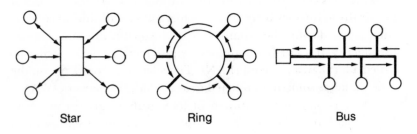

| Star | Ring | Bus |

Ring networks do have this connectivity, as each sender's message finds its recipient by passing the intervening stations (not going through some central switch). Bus networks work similarly: While a bus has a special device at the head end of the cable to reflect incoming signals outward along the same cable, this "remodulator" typically costs only one or two thousand dollars and does not have or need any routing intelligence.

To be a LAN, a network must have full connectivity among stations, be fully administered by the owner (and not the FCC), and run on a single set of cables. The second and third parts of this definition eliminate commercial CATV networks and any dialup facility operating over a common carrier. Although the telephonic wide area network does not qualify as a LAN, every local device up to and including the connecting modem might, as seen in Figure 1.2.

LANs may be categorized as general purpose, special purpose, and proprietary. A proprietary LAN, while satisfying the basic definition above, has the disadvantage of being incompatible with the products of other vendors, thus locking the owner into one vendor's hardware and software. Nonproprietary LANs may be developed for a single purpose: for example, to connect robot controllers and other devices of various vendors to accomplish the task of painting an automobile. General purpose LANs, while sometimes developed to serve a limited use, are capable of supporting a variety of vendors' devices and application software.

Figure 1.2 WAN-centered and LAN-centered viewpoints.

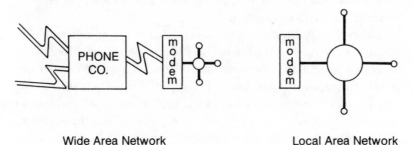

Wide Area Network   Local Area Network

THE NEED FOR STANDARDS

Late in the 1970s, both IEEE and ANSI saw the need for at least some broad standard hierarchy, so that the same vendor would not have to supply both the hardware device connecting the PC or robot or word processor to the network and the software commands used by a program or operator to receive a signal from another station on the network. Appropriate committees produced standards.

The intelligent entity doing the communicating was called an open system, and the seven-layer standard produced by ANSI was termed the OSI (Open Systems Interconnection) Reference Model.

THE OSI MODEL

Figure 1.3 illustrates the seven layers in the OSI standard for LANs. Going from the bottom upward, the formal names of these layers are the Physical, Data Link, Network, Transport, Session, Presentation, and Application Layers. At least in principle, a LAN designer could select a different hardware or software supplier for each of these seven LAN functions. In practice, a given product may address several of these needs at once, but the OSI model still has the benefit that the vendor must make at least some allowance for compatibility of that product with others in the layers not addressed.

It is worthwhile to learn the names of the seven layers, as they are now an integral part of the vocabulary of LANs. Explanatory sales brochures, and even some business contracts now make explicit reference to the OSI layers in discussing what services are (and are not) performed by a given product.

Layer 7: Application. This layer is easily comprehensible to anyone who has worked with a PC, graphics machine, word processor, programmable controller, or robot. Layer 7 does not carry out the application itself, but rather supplies functions such as file transfer or electronic mail by which the program or workstation operator communicates with other "open systems" on the network.

For example, application programs in the PC DOS operating system use the command "PRINT" to activate a printer handwired to

Figure 1.3 Open Systems Interconnection (OSI) model.

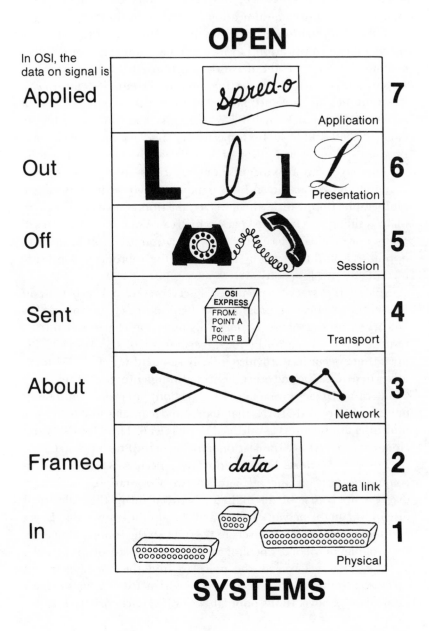

OPEN

In OSI, the data on signal is

Applied	*spred-o* · Application	**7**
Out	L ℓ l 𝓛 · Presentation	**6**
Off	Session	**5**
Sent	OSI EXPRESS / FROM: POINT A / To: POINT B · Transport	**4**
About	Network	**3**
Framed	*data* · Data link	**2**
In	Physical	**1**

SYSTEMS

that PC. To use a shared printer accessed through the LAN, the Microsoft Networks product requires the command "NET PRINT." In many cases, the communication is nearly that simple.

Layer 6: Presentation. One step lower, this layer has the job of seeing that an Application Layer command is translated into syntax common throughout the network and translated back upward to Layer 7 once it reaches its destination. Microcomputer enthusiasts, for example, are well acquainted with the ASCII translation of commands (ACK-acknowledge receipt) and text ("A") into binary data (1000001 and 0000110, respectively) and back out again. Compression and some encryption of data also are functions of Layer 6.

This layer can also disguise one device as another to improve economy and/or security. A PC program may believe that it is using a (vulnerable) floppy disk when, in fact, the storage area is one of very many residing on a large diskpack, which can economically be backed up to tape on a daily basis. Or the workstation itself can be made to appear as a 3270 terminal by interposing the appropriate hardware ("emulator" card) or software.

Shared resources—especially fileservers—are a key benefit of LANs. But application programs written before networking need to be adapted for shared use so competing users don't harm each other's results. Since its release in 1984, Version 3.1 of the MS-DOS PC operating system has provided a fairly standard way for IBM look-alikes to request file and other services (through program "Interrupt" 21). Because DOS 3.1 (or a later DOS version) can protect entire files or individual records, LANs that understand it are able to synchronize multiuser applications as outlined in Chapter 6. Thus, for IBMs and clones, it can serve as a translation standard at the Presentation Layer.

Layer 5: Session. The Session Layer decides when to turn a communication on and off between two workstations. It actively oversees the course of the dialogue between them. If an electrical disruption on the network temporarily breaks the connection, Layer 5 can often get the lower layers to re-establish the connection before the program or robot or operator at either end is aware of any trouble.

The Session Layer is the place to find the one widespread exception to the rule that each layer be instructed only by the layer immediately above. IBM's popular NETBIOS (Network Basic Input

Output Services) software can convey Layer 5 commands from either DOS or an application (through program "interrupt" 5C) in establishing a session via CALL and LISTEN or terminating it via HANG UP.

Layer 4: Transport. Similarly, the Transport Layer ensures that data passed upward to it is sent successfully. It establishes and maintains the connection and has the responsibility of demanding a retransmission if notified that the data frame or packet (see Layer 2, below) did not arrive intact.

Layer 3: Network. In Layers 7, 6, 5, and 4, it is assumed that the sent signal somehow has gotten around the LAN and arrived at the designated node. The Network Layer is responsible for translating logical addresses (that is, names) into physical addresses and for picking the best network route if more than one is available on that LAN.

In a network with many branches, this second task of Layer 3 is very significant. But within the simpler topologies, its main internal task is to keep and convey statistics about the LAN; for example, which stations are disabled. An important external task, usually done at Layer 3, is to connect the LAN to non-OSI networks or machines, using interface devices called protocol converters or gateways.

Layer 2: Data link. Layer 2 is responsible for getting the data packaged and onto the cable successfully. When other layers give it a sending address and receiving address and data, Layer 2 reshapes the data into standard blocks and sets up a "frame" or "packet" to convey each block. At the other end, Layer 2 notifies Transport (Layer 4) if something is wrong with the packet.

Figure 1.4 shows some of the standard packet (frame) formats, which may also include leading bytes for synchronization and check bytes to ensure data integrity. These two control features are condensed for non-LAN "asynchronous" byte transmission between entities hardwired to each other: No addresses are needed and a single bit is used for error checking. It is turned on or off so as to make the total bit count ("parity") odd. In place of a "sync" byte, there is an extra "off" bit to start and stop each byte.

In asynchronous communications, the sender must wait for an ACK before sending the next byte. With protocols such as Synchro-

Figure 1.4 Asynchronous and synchronous frames.

Start bit (off)	Seven-bit ASCII Symbol	Check bit	Stop bit (off)

SDLC frame:

Start flag 01111110	Address byte	Control byte	Data Bytes	Two Check bytes	End flag 01111110

Ethernet frame:

Sync	Dest Address byte	Source Address byte	Packet Type 2 bytes	Data Bytes	Cyclic Check 2 bytes

nous Data Link Control (SDLC), the recipient may receive seven or more multibyte frames before responding—and is allowed to send at the same time. Finally, two or more LANs with the same frame size and addressing scheme can be connected at Layer 2 by a device called a *bridge.*

Layer 1: Physical. This layer gets the bits in and conveys them. The transmission line can support a broad set of signals, each merging its binary information with a specific transmitting wave. Alternatively, the entire line can be occupied by one basic binary signal.

A Layer 1 "baseband" system uses a signal line with a specified base voltage ("off") and then varies the voltage to show an "on" bit for each specified period of time. This network signaling resembles the bit flow that occurs along a fixed direct connection between a personal computer and its printer or other device.

In a particular industry-wide standard (RS232C), the transmission of data involves a real electric current, with "off" bits a positive 15 volts and "on" bits a negative 15 volts. Because of line loss, the signal threshhold is +/- 5V for outgoing and only +/- 3V for incoming signals: Anything closer to zero is ambiguous. The typical Ethernet baseband LAN also uses a voltage change to signify a bit flip, although base voltages may differ.

For basebands using a coaxial cable bus, each "open system" taps into the LAN through a transmittor/receiver (transreceiver), which either is spliced into the cable ("obtrusive" T-connector) or digs a metal pin through insulating material to reach to the center wire (vampire tap).

In contrast to baseband, a "broadband" line may have many conversations going on simultaneously on different channels, a process known as frequency division multiplexing (FDM). No real electricity flows, only TV-like oscillations along the surface of the cable. Whereas digital devices can use transceivers to splice directly into a baseband system, broadband requires a more costly "modem" on each network interface unit (NIU) to make the transition from raw bits to the analog "carrier" frequencies shown in Figure 1.5, and back again.

The large total frequency bandwidth of broadband systems permits multiple simultaneous transmissions of voice, video and data on the same cable, through dividing the electromagnetic spectrum into distinct channels with frequency intervals of 50 KHz for voice and 6 MHz for video. This is called Frequency Division Multiplexing (FDM).

In LAN terminology, there are two distinct meanings for the word "bandwidth." The sense just used, namely size of a channel in terms of its highest minus its lowest frequency, is historically the original

Figure 1.5 The broadband spectrum.

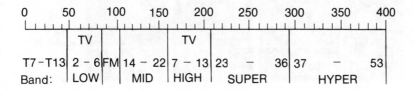

Broadband Frequencies and CATV Channels
(In MegaHerz)

meaning of the word. But even when FDM is not involved, often "bandwidth" is used to indicate the rate at which data bits can go through a LAN. In that case the units are bits per second (b/s), not cycles per second (Hz or KHz or MHz).

Whenever a "carrier" frequency is used to transmit data, the two meanings are linked. A low-speed transmission may transmit only 9.6 Kb/s, over a bandwidth of approximately 50 KHz. Ethernet may transmit several Mb/s over a single TV-width channel (6 MHz). And the aggregate data rate that a full broadband cable can support, reaches into the hundreds of megabits per second.

To distinguish the signal from the medium it traverses, sometimes, the physical wiring and connectors are referred to as "Layer 0."

ARBITRATING USE OF THE NETWORK

Layer 1 also governs the sharing ("arbitration") of the line among stations. The "802" Committee of the IEEE has specified standards for three different methods of line sharing: Token Passing Ring (802.5), Token Passing Bus (802.4), and Carrier Sensing Multiple Access (802.2). Both CSMA and token passing are forms of time division multiplexing (TDM), the taking of turns. See Figure 1.6.

Figure 1.6 IEEE 802 LAN standards.

IEEE-802 Family

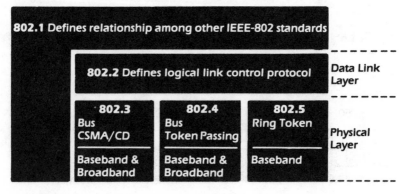

Arbitration by Token (Ring or Bus)

In a token ring LAN, such as IBM announced in October 1985, a special byte is circulated about the network. If station A has this token, it can attach addressing information and data to it and request a service from C. The packet leaves station B's buffer area without harm because B does not see its name in the packet. C receives the packet and sends back a frame that is nearly identical but has a "received" bit turned on. D passes this along, and when A receives it and verifies that the data was received intact, A places a fresh token on the network so that another node can transmit. See Figure 1.7. If a node becomes disabled, it can be bypassed by Layer 3 or it may have a physical bypass path built into the hardware.

Although IEEE 802.5 uses ring topology and 802.4 uses bus topology (a sort of flattened ring), both of these specifications call for use of a token. Arbitration by token is deterministic because each node in turn will eventually receive the token. As long as the number of nodes does not become huge, the 1/30,000 second in-and-out time per node does no real harm. But it may become important in the case of a milling machine, where adjustments must be made in times approximately one thousandth of a second.

Arbitration by Listening (Bus)

IEEE 802.3 specifies a bus in which use of the line is arbitrated by a tape of "listening," known as Carrier Sensing Multiple Access with

Figure 1.7 IEEE 802.5 token passing ring.

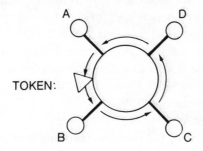

Collison Detection (CSMA/CD). Each node's broadcast reaches all nodes, not just the addressee.

In some ways, CSMA/CD is analogous to having a room full of people who all want to speak but must first listen to see if someone else is speaking. At each node the transreceiver "listens" by measuring whether or not the cable stays at the base voltage for several microseconds at a time (9.8 μ sec for IEEE 802.3).

In CSMA/CD, any station may place a packet on the unoccupied network and wait to receive back an echo. If the echo is identical to what was sent, that station knows that the message got through. If the echo differs, it and at least one other station know that a collision has occurred. After a specified "backoff" time, each node sends again. Since the delays differ for each node, success is likely the next time—unless there is so much work to be done that collisions are happening constantly.

MAP AND TOP: SPECIALIZED FACTORY AND OFFICE STANDARDS

Token Bus (IEEE 802.4) and CSMA/CD Bus (IEEE 802.3) are perhaps best suited for different uses. Token passing fits the factory, and CSMA/CD fits the office.

A factory cell may have few stations with frequent signaling, and so the small delay per station becomes less crucial than the guarantee that each station will have chance to transmit before one preceding it on line gets to send a second message. A new factory-oriented set of specifications, Manufacturing Automation Protocol (MAP) is thus based on 802.4.

On the other hand, an office LAN may have very many stations with relatively infrequent network requests. Here the time to get around the network (if regenerating a token at each node) could prove prohibitive. Since office workers do not usually all submit their network requests at exactly the same time, the loss due to collisions might be tolerated. Thus 802.3 forms the basic for the emerging Technical and Office Protocol (TOP).

The selection of CSMA/CD as the TOP standard should not deter the reader from considering the more recently implemented token ring (IEEE 802.5) in office settings.

In their respective professional and industrial groups, the MAP/TOP committees envision the day when the two sets of OSI protocols are completely formulated and become international standards. For MAP, the earlier of the two, full factory implementation was targeted to occur by 1990.

MAP enthusiasts point out that codification and widespread acceptance can generate a large enough market for the economical manufacture of VLSI products that reduce OSI Layers 1 through 4 to hardware. Some MAP partisans feel that this effort can leapfrog the United States to a five-year lead over other nations known for the automation and coordination of their factories.

The first publicized large-scale MAP demonstration took place at the 1985 Autofact convention in Detroit. MAP was demonstrated in conjunction with many different kinds of computers and factory machines. The external unit attached to all devices on the LAN was Concord Data Systems' TIM (Token/Net Interface Module), which provided token bus services over broadband at five million bits of information per second. Allen-Bradley was chosen to supply the gateway to non-OSI systems. We should remember that these were not the only MAP suppliers at that time, and, as with all aspects of LANs, the vendor list is still growing.

Richard G. Lefkon
Citibank, N.A.

Donald R. DiBrita
Nestar Systems, Inc.

William Berkman
Orchid Technologies

2

Some Thoughts on Planning a LAN

Regardless of the size of the anticipated local area network, those who are planning the system will want to keep a number of general principles in mind. Let's look, first, at some of the key principles, then at how they apply to the selection of equipment.

• *Wiring:* Coaxial or fiber should be used where appropriate (between floors, between buildings, through harsh environments), but simple twisted-pair can often be used elsewhere. If fiber is used, LED sources are preferred over lasers on the basis of both cost and reliability. See Figure 2.1.

• *Availability:* There should be clear and effective procedures for network use (and repair). Some LAN products provide good availability by having a central interface that can tell a monitor where

Figure 2.1 Varied cabling for Proteon's rings.

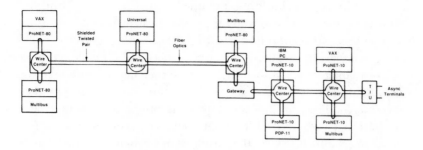

and of what nature the problems are. Even better is a network manager station that can actively subdivide and diagnose a sick LAN while it is still running.

- *Reliability:* The network should have a high mean-time-between-failures measure. Procedures should be established to avoid the confusion and human error that causes most system problems. Interconnecting cabling should be in the hands of professionals, since most problems not caused by human error are in the media themselves.

- *Maintainability:* The LAN must have a short mean-time-to-repair. Hardware layouts should be simple and obvious, using color-coding wherever appropriate. Control of activity during the repair is key. Finally, backup and archiving procedures should be well-established by the time the first user attempts to log on.

- *Flexibility:* The network layout should be designed for expansion. Taps off the network should be added generously to allow for evolution and reconfigurations of the network. A network that places too many restrictions on run length, number of bypassed (failed) nodes, and the like should be scrutinized very carefully, with worst-case conditions in mind. Loading should also be considered as a function of traffic, whether "bursty" terminal traffic, or sustained data transmissions.

- *Physical Plant:* Networks can be reconfigured more easily if there are distribution panels or patch boxes. These permit users to be added or moved by re-attaching local "lobes." There has been a conscious move by some high-tech building developers toward "intelligent buildings," i.e., buildings designed to give network cabling and ports the same priority as water pipes and heating ducts.

• *Interdepartmental Planning:* LANs can integrate voice, video and data sharing. Perhaps only one is needed by the department whose manager is reading this book. Other departments may be willing to share expenses. Even if they are not, their input should be encouraged. This can prevent their being offended when they later discover that a key need has been ignored, as in planning one too few incoming channels to serve the corporation's two- to five-year plan. A specific technique for involving other departments is explained in the Appendix.

• *Unanticipated Uses:* A recent American Management Association survey of information centers showed that the corporations themselves planned a 40 percent increase in the number of personal computers they would own in the one-year period following publication of this book! Even more striking is the finding that the number of networked PCs would rise by 100 percent (double) in the same one-year period.

Few of these workstations or networks will be limited permanently to the tasks anticipated before actual installation. LANs acquired for word processing and electronic mail somehow seem to wind up providing graphics and spreadsheets and simulations as well. Hardware can be as unanticipated as software: A Dataquest survey has shown that although most small LANs were purchased to help share storage, fully one quarter of them today are sharing laser printers among the workstations.

DON'T IGNORE BASEBAND BECAUSE OF STATUS

Baseband LANs tend to be less expensive than broadband LANs, in part because the latter have many more "bells and whistles." But there is nothing wrong with selecting a LAN on the basis of how well it does its job. In some cases, baseband will prove the better choice. It can often support the desired services equally well. See Figure 2.2.

An average baseband LAN transmits 2.5 million bits per second

Figure 2.2 Nestar's "linked stars" configuration for baseband or broadband.

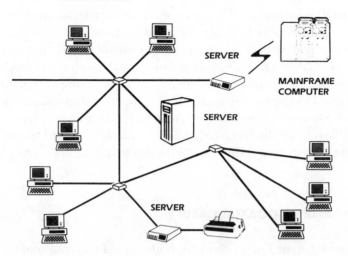

(Mb/s). Typical LAN products achieve transmission speeds of one to ten megabits (Mb/s) of binary data, occupying the entire available bandwidth. Some of the more sophisticated basebands can support one hundred megabits.

The installation of baseband or any other type of metal cabling is physically very much the same, with one major exception: Adding a baseband node is as simple as tapping into the carrier. Considerations in a broadband system include making sure all the cable components are functioning with an electrical impedance of 75 ohms.

IBM's first local network product, the PC Network, running under IBM PC DOS 2.1, was a broadband implementation. The cables used were pretuned for simplicity, but that also meant restrictions, such as fixed lengths. The October 1985 token ring announcement uses instead a baseband LAN design.

The ability to tap into the wiring plant at any point along its path makes the initial task of wiring baseband layouts mistake-free. Any necessary changes or oversights in preinstallation can be corrected quickly. More extensive planning is needed for broadband systems, coupled with the requirement for splitters, tuners, and hardware kits.

COMBINE BASEBAND AND BROADBAND

A baseband signal may interface with or support a broadband system, providing a series of flexible alternatives. One possibility is to use a broadband cable, already in place within a physical installation, as a "backbone." A preexisting broadband running through a building's central wiring shaft might be used for linking all floors together, with individual floors wired for baseband to support group clusters or workstations and uncomplicated growth. Whether over cable or optical fiber, many distinct baseband LANs can be conveyed among floors via corresponding channels of the full frequency spectrum.

TWISTED PAIR VS. COAXIAL CABLE

There are inherent limitations with both twisted pair and coaxial. The primary difference between the two is shielding. Twisted pair has no form of shielding against radio frequency interference (RFI). By contrast, coaxial does have a protective shield around the primary conductor.

Twisted pair, also known as telco or telephone wire, typically has two individual pairs (four independent strands) surrounded by a flexible rubberized plastic insulation. It works well in low data speed environments and is very cost-effective. Installation is usually quite easy, due to the flexibility and small size of the cable. Distance, speed, and RFI are normally limiting factors of twisted pair.

One of the primary concerns in installing a cable for data communication is physical flexibility. Consider what happens when the cable has to turn a hard corner. Twisted pair can be routed around door jambs and through right angle conduits. Coaxial, on the other hand, is limited in this regard, usually requiring a turn diameter of four to six inches.

Another advantage of twisted pair is the size of the cable. Telephone wire is very small, less than an eighth of an inch in diameter. Coax ranges from a quarter of an inch to three quarters of an inch.

Thus twisted pair can fit into nearly any place desired, whereas coax must be treated with caution and its placement within an office may be limited.

Coaxial cable, however, is often superior in aspects other than physical flexibility and cost. Coaxial has a protective shield consisting of a wire braid or foil wrap, or sometimes both. Because of the shield, coaxial is able to carry much higher frequencies and data rates than twisted pair. A typical coax LAN can transmit up to ten million bits per second (Mb/s), whereas the (unshielded) twisted pair is limited to approximately one Mb/s. (Shielded twisted pair presents a compromise in terms of cost and throughput.)

Coaxial not only carries more information than twisted pair, it carries it greater distances. The thicker the cable, the better. Cable differences are easily seen in the relative distance performance of Orchid Technology's PCnet LAN. This product can cover 7,000 feet end-to-end when run on heavy gauge (RG-11/U) coaxial cable. But with thinner coaxial (RG-59-U), it can only cover 3,000 feet.

The ability to carry more data and a variety of signals over large distances is the main justification for the increased cost of the shielding of coax. Typically, coaxial costs three to five times as much as twisted pair.

Chapter 3 deals with baseband LANs, often associated with twisted pair (or at least the thinner RG-59/U coaxial). Chapter 4 describes in detail the use of various grades of cable in conjunction with broadband LANs. Chapter 5 examines optical fiber LANs, in which the cabling medium has some of the good properties of both coaxial and twisted pair.

Bruce D. Schatzman
Xerox Corporation

3

A Practical Look at Baseband

The majority of LANs now used in offices utilize baseband technology. Flexible and relatively simple, baseband can support an exceedingly wide range of equipment, configurations and topologies. Dozens of companies, including Xerox, DEC, Intel, Interlan and 3Com manufacture a wide range of baseband products.

The software offerings are equally diverse, providing different levels of sophistication to suit different environments. Small work groups of PCs need only limited functionality and may be completely satisfied by file sharing, printer sharing and electronic mail. Larger networks may require a vast array of services, and for these needs there are more sophisticated solutions available.

The key is understanding not just what is needed but also what is not needed.

TECHNICAL BACKGROUND

The distinguishing characteristic of baseband networks is the way in which data travels across the communications medium (such as coaxial cable). In baseband technology, data is pulsed directly onto the medium in digital format at a rate matching the specified data transfer speed of the network. Text, graphics and other information is reduced to a stream of 1's and 0's (presence or absence of a signal) on the communications medium. Typically, one channel is used for all data traffic, meaning that there is essentially a one-lane "freeway" on which data can travel.

The other primary network technology, broadband, uses a radio frequency modulator/demodulator (modem) to send data in RF (analog) format. This format allows multiple channels and makes it suitable for different applications.

Baseband networks typically support a data transmission rate in the 9 to 10 Mb/s (mega BITs per second) range, with actual throughout in the 0 to 4 Mb/s range. That is, while many baseband networks transmit data in short bursts up to 10 Mb/s, actual end-to-end data exchange averages out to the lower figure for large amounts of data over long periods of time.

There are two basic "arbitration methods" used in baseband networks: contention (CSMA/CD) and token passing (see Chapter 1). The manner in which these access methods operate implies another characteristic of baseband networks: Only one device can transmit data at any particular instant. The relatively high speed of a baseband, however, gives the illusion that many devices are sending data simultaneously because several transmissions can occur in just a few seconds.

NODE AND DISTANCE LIMITS

Because of their relative simplicity and flexibility, baseband networks are practical for tying together a small or large number of devices. A low-cost, twisted pair (telephone wire) baseband network may support only 100 devices but will suffice for a small group of PCs while technologies such as Ethernet can support up to 1,024 devices on a single network. It is possible to connect separate Ethernet networks via a device known as a bridge (see Chapter 7), and that can extend the total number of devices into the tens of thousands. However, the use of a bridge usually penalizes performance.

Low-cost networks may be restricted to as short as 250 meters of cable, while the more sophisticated ones allow up to 4 kilometers (Km) on fiber optic cable. This is sufficient to wire fully most office buildings. Linking physically remote LANs may involve greater distances, such as interbuilding, interstate or international. For these, microwave transmitters, satellite links or dedicated high speed telephone lines can be used to span the intervening distance.

SERVERS AND SHARED RESOURCES

A variety of network "architectures" such as Xerox Network Systems (XNS), DEC's Digital Network Architecture (DNA) and Boeing's Technical and Office Protocols (TOP) are available on baseband hardware.

The applications and services offered are often supported by dedicated devices called servers, which attach to networks in the same manner as any other computing device. They facilitate resource sharing by offering better performance and low overall costs. The server can be a PC, workstation, minicomputer or other computing device containing appropriate software. Servers are the heart of shared resources, and understanding what they do is vital to appreciating how a LAN functions:

• *File Server:* Usually a computer with a large-capacity drive attached internally or externally. It gives users shared access to large file storage and cuts costs by reducing the need for expensive disk drives at each workstation. This centralizing of data makes security and backup easier to manage.

• *Database Server:* A device dedicated to running database software and maintaining the database itself. Database management is CPU-intensive, and many devices (such as PCs) do not have the power to handle some of the more sophisticated software. It is best, then, to offload this task to a computer designed for this responsibility.

• *Directory Server:* Stores and maintains lists of users and network resources. Sometimes called a clearinghouse, it can be used as "yellow pages" to help users identify what resources (such as printers) are available and how they can be accessed.

• *Print Server:* Offloads printing chores from other nodes. It allows document printing to be accomplished "off-line" while the user goes on to accomplish other tasks.

• *Communications Server:* Usually responsible for shared communications such as gateways to other networks (see Chapter 8), internetwork routing, and asynchronous (RS-232) logon to remote hosts using a modem.

• *Mail Server:* All electronic mail is usually processed by this device before being routed to its final destination. Mail servers maintain names and network addresses for authorized users and ensure reliable mail transfer by checking name and address acccuracy before message delivery.

This list represents just a few of the more popular types. With appropriate software, a server can be set up to handle almost any task that is outside the responsibility of the typical user node.

BASEBAND LAN EXAMPLES

Figure 3.1 shows a low-cost network based on twisted-pair wiring, suitable for small work groups of PCs with relatively simple needs. The LAN can support up to 150 nodes. Maximum transmission

Figure 3.1 Simple twisted pair network.

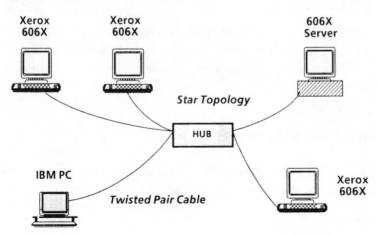

Figure 3.2 Use of RG 58 cabling.

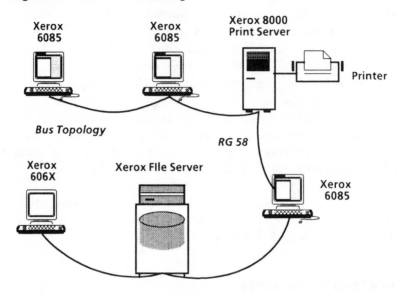

speed is 1 Mb/s over an AT&T STARLAN topology.

Figure 3.2 illustrates the use of thin coaxial (RG-58/U) cabling to satisfy the needs of a more sophisticated work group involving more powerful machines. Note the direct connection of the cable to the devices without the need for transceivers and drop cables as with standard coaxial. Transmission speed is 10 Mb/s, and literally hundreds of nodes are supported in this version of Ethernet.

Figure 3.3 shows the use of standard Ethernet in a larger network. Note the use of drop cables and transceivers and the interconnection of two networks (A and B) via a bridge running inside a communications server.

COMPARISON WITH BROADBAND

Any technology has its limits. There are a variety of situations which require the integration of text, graphics, voice, and video within the same carrier. This is particularly difficult for baseband systems to

Figure 3.3 Large Ethernet network.

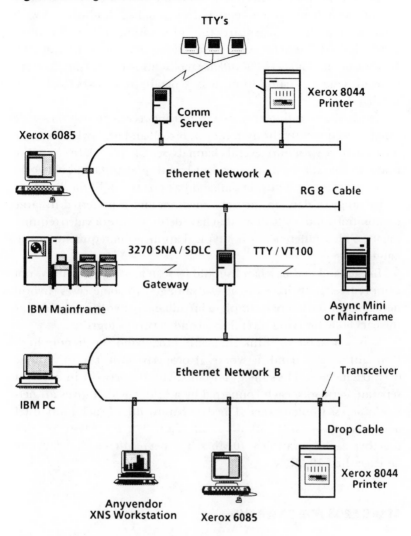

handle, primarily because the decomposition of voice and video to 1's and 0's results in huge amounts of binary data. The representation of a single color video image in digital format may require upwards of a megabyte of information.

Broadband is able effectively to handle voice and video data by dealing with them in their "native" form (analog). Radio waves with relatively high frequencies carry this information through the medium without the need for conversion to long sequences of 1's and 0's. Because broadband needs frequency modulation devices (modems) to transmit data in analog form, it is generally more expensive than baseband.

Just as radio equipment can transmit and receive signals on a wide range of frequencies through the air, broadband networks allow the medium to be split into several channels (see Chapter 4). In effect, the coaxial cable can be divided as if it had several baseband networks running inside it. Thus, broadband has greater ability to handle a wider range of data on the same medium and is preferred in large corporations and institutions that have definite voice or video requirements. Videoconferencing is a typical application requiring broadband.

Broadband and baseband should be seen as complementary, not competitive. Both have distinct advantages. In some cases, hybrid networks are built. For example, a broadband network can be used as the backbone for tying several baseband networks together.

It is a mistake to think that only broadband can handle high throughput. Baseband networks, if properly built, can offer huge overall data rates. The strategy is to subdivide the network into several separate networks, each connected by a bridge which gives all networks access to each other. The data bandwidth of each individual network cannot exceed 10 Mb/s, but many data freeways can work together, each operating at 10 Mb/s. The net result is a total data rate far exceeding 10 Mb/s.

STANDARDS FOR BASEBAND

OSI Layers 1 and 2 are made specific by the "802" standards of the Institute of Electrical and Electronics Engineers. The IEEE 802.3 (CSMA/CD) and 802.5 (token ring) standards for baseband have created stability in what otherwise would have been a chaotic baseband LAN market. They give manufacturers a set of specifications by which their products can at least connect at the two lowest layers.

The more mature one, IEEE 802.3, was developed jointly by Xerox, Digital Equipment and Intel under the name Ethernet. Work on it began as early as 1972 at Xerox' Palo Alto Research Center. The first edition of this standard, IEEE 802.3-1985, defines a 10 Mb/s baseband using CSMA/CD arbitration.

Most current LAN products based on OSI implement only the first four layers (Physical through Transport) and therefore have limited functionality. What can be done—in the absence of standards —to implement the higher layers? One interim solution is for computer manufacturers to adopt de facto standards that are publicly available.

There are at least two complete standard schemes: DARPA (TCP/IP), developed by U. C. Berkeley for the Department of Defense, and XNS, developed by Xerox. Both are publicly available as they are included in versions of UNIX offered by Berkeley. Since they are embedded in the C language and thus can be used on computers running C, both "architectures" should see increasing implementation by computer manufacturers.

Chapter 9 gives a UNIX example and discusses IBM communication protocols. Industry-wide office standards are treated in Chapter 11.

THE FUTURE

Many corporations that produce network products are conducting research on how to extend baseband technology far beyond its present capacity. Already, products are available using sophisticated transceivers or fiber optic media (see Chapter 5) that increase the available data rates from their present 10 Mb/s range to 100 Mb/s and more. New semiconductor devices promise to increase performance by implementing more OSI layers in hardware, while other development projects are underway which may be able to integrate voice within baseband networks.

Oleh Maczaj
Richard G. Lefkon
Citibank, N.A.

4

Broadband Diversity and Cabling

Broadband LANs have their origins in CATV, community antenna television systems which used coaxial cable to route video and audio signals from a master antenna to home receivers some distance away. The technology used there has matured and become more sophisticated, today having many suppliers and competitive pricing. See Figure 4.1.

Figure 4.1 Diverse signals on UB's Net 1 broadband.

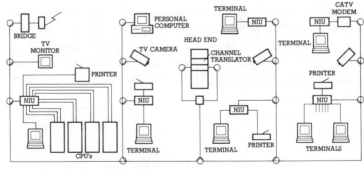

TWO-WAY CHANNELS OF COAXIAL CABLE

Originally, CATV systems were designed for uni-directional (broadcast) information distribution. Over time, they evolved the capability for bi-directional information traffic by setting aside the lower part of the frequency bandwidth for signals traveling in the other direction.

A "headend remodulator" allows any two points on the LAN to communicate by retransmitting signals back away from itself. It receives any particular low frequency signal and raises it by a fixed amount before retransmitting out onto the network. The old CATV terminology has stuck, and so "forward" signals are those that travel away from the headend, while incoming signals are said to travel in "reverse."

There are four fairly standard extents to which incoming channels are carved out of the full frequency spectrum shown in Figure 4.2:

- *Sub-split:* 5 to 30 MHz (4 incoming channels) in the reverse direction, 50 to 408 MHz (58 outbound channels) in the forward direction.
- *Mid-split:* 5 to 108 MHz (17 channels) reverse, 156 to 408 MHz (42 channels) forward.
- *High-split:* 5 to 186 MHz (29 channels) reverse, 222 to 450 MHz (30 channels) forward.

Figure 4.2 Channel allocations on broadband.

IEEE-802 Family

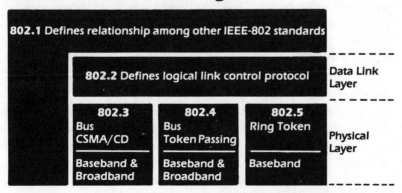

- *Dual cable:* 42 to 408 MHz (59 channels) over each of two parallel cables, one reverse and the other forward. This is the only case of true equality.

Just how each headend remodulator converts incoming to outgoing signals is made clear by this simple example from mid-split broadband: Using a channel 5 to channel S headend remodulator, the device listens for messages on channel 5 and boosts the frequency just enough to send the same data back out again on channel S.

Careful evaluation of present requirements—and some imaginative speculation over future requirements—should be done prior to installing a broadband LAN. Video (closed circuit TV) uses up the most bandwidth per channel. Next, consideration should be given to data and voice requirements. Here the reader should be guided by the availability of particular devices and the channels (frequencies) they will function on. Only after analyzing both the bi-directional needs as well as the likely equipment should the reader decide which type of frequency split to choose: Sub, Mid, High, or Dual Cable.

ELECTRICAL PROPERTIES

A broadband network consists of several types of components in addition to the cable itself. These can be categorized broadly as being "active" or "passive."

Passive components comprise all the non-powered components that are part of the cable plant. This includes taps, splitters, couplers, combiners, equalizers and terminators. These devices may pass electrical power through to other components on the cable, but they do not need electricity to do their own jobs. Active devices, such as amplifiers, need power to function, usually drawn from a 30 or 60 volt AC supply.

The electrical standards for the cable itself and the active and passive components are very well defined. Broadband networks make use of 75 Ohm impedance cable. These cables are usually designated with an RG-xx number for the smaller gauge cables (such as RG-59/U, RG-11/U and RG-6/U) or by the cable diameter (such as .5 inch and .75 inch).

Figure 4.3 Six common kinds of broadband cable.

Description	Outer Diameter	Center Conductor	Signal Loss (db/100ft)*
.75 jacketed	.75 inch	.169 inch	.16/.50/1.7
.5 jacketed	.5	.111	.23/.74/2.4
.5 unjacketed	.5	.111	.23/.74/2.4
RG 11/U	.4	.037	.45/1.3/4.5
RG 6/U	.275	.037	.80/2.1/6.8
RG 59/U	.24	.025	1.0/2.5/8.8

*Signal loss figures in the last column are for
frequencies of 10 Mhz, 100 Mhz and 1000 Mhz.

Figure 4.3 lists six common kinds of broadband cable. Even though they all have 75 Ohms impedance, their signal loss per foot (attenuation) varies according to their diameter. Attenuation is measured in decibels (db); three decibels loss corresponds to signal reduction by a factor of ten. The thicker the center conductor, the lower the signal loss per foot. Also, higher frequency signals are attenuated more than lower frequencies on the same diameter cable. This attenuation-with-frequency relationship is shown in the graph in Figure 4.4.

Less obvious is the attenuation difference between the 11/U and 6/U coax shown in the table. The 11/U loses less signal because its outer shield is farther away from the center (.4 inch outer diameter vs. .275 inch). Thus the outer shield comes in contact less with the rapidly changing electromagnetic field surrounding the center conductor and steals away less of its energy.

Actual choice of cable is usually dictated by the environment and the complexity of the network. Only the smallest networks would consist entirely of any of the RG-xx cable due to its high loss characteristics. Instead the use of this class of cable is reserved for local clusters which are then attached to .5-inch or .75-inch trunk cable.

Figure 4.4 Signal loss rises with frequency.

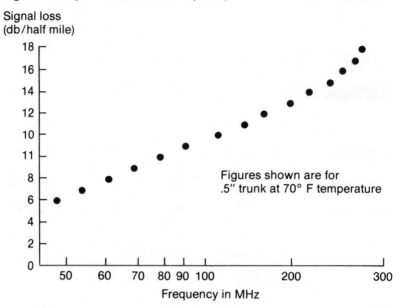

Signal loss
(db/half mile)

Frequency in MHz

Figures shown are for
.5" trunk at 70° F temperature

CABLE PLACEMENT

The more knowledgeable and involved the reader becomes with broadband cabling and other LAN considerations, the better the resulting local area network.

It is wise to make the LAN cable bypass areas likely to have repeated work by telephone or electrical contractors since such work may damage the cabling. A decision as simple as running the cable a foot away from the usual tangle of telephone and electrical wires (and keeping it there by tying it down every few feet) can avoid disruption of network services due to construction activities.

Cable selection should also be based on the degree to which it will be exposed to EMI, the elements, and rodents. For instance, the soft RG-xx coaxial should be limited to indoor use away from harsh environments.

Trunk cabling (.5 and .75 inch) is manufactured with or without a protective PVC plastic jacket covering the solid aluminum shield. This jacket helps to protect against corrosion, dents and kinks in the aluminum shield. Not only is this cable resistant to hungry rodents, but there are jelly-filled waterproof versions for below ground installation.

Indoors, if EMI is present (near airports or radio/TV transmission antennas), the most heavily shielded (quadshield) versions of RG-xx cables should be used. Their multiple foil and braid shields keep out electromagnetic noise better than a single-braided wire shield.

Many municipalities have fire codes that restrict the kind of jacketing and internal insulation a cable can use. Often PVC (a suspected carcinogen when burning) is prohibited in ceiling or air vent installation. Half-inch trunk cable using "fused disk" teflon filler costs approximately twice as much as the foam dielectric version. Teflon versions of RG-xx cables may run as high as six times the cost of the PVC kind.

Thus the choice of the cable to be used in the LAN is dictated in part by its size, but also in part by the environment. An example of how different grades of cable might be used in a multibuilding (factory or campus) network is as follows:

- .75-inch jacketed coax linking the various buildings.
- .5-inch unjacketed coax used as a trunk for distribution within each building.
- RG-59 cable linking devices to LAN taps within each building.
- RG-11 (thicker than RG-59) within the headend to link the various components (translator, combiners, and the like) and avoid signal loss or EMI among them.

The loss attributed to the cable and passive components needs to be overcome if the network is to function. This loss can be compensated for through the use of amplifiers that raise the signal level in such a way (slope) that the loss in higher frequency signals is replenished more than the smaller loss of low-frequency signals.

This process is less complicated on a baseband network since there is not a range of frequencies, and the single digital signal can in principle simply be amplified by retransmission using a "repeater" and sent down the next span of wire or cable.

Because amplifiers amplify all signals including background noise, there are limits on how many places a shrinking signal can be amplified before the "signal to noise ratio" grows too small.

Albert D. Bender
FiberCom, Inc.

Richard G. Lefkon
New York University

5

Optical Fiber: Truth amid Blue Sky

The need for fiber optical networks has already risen to meet their declining cost curve. A light emitting diode that cost $200 several years ago now can be bought for less than $10. The arrival of LANs with their high bandwidth requirement (10 Mb/s for Ethernet and 4 or 16 Mb/s for IBM Token) has focused attention on fiber, which has much less signal loss than coaxial cable for these and wider bandwidths.

Typical fibers are thinner (three millimeters), lighter (55 pounds per fiber mile), more flexible, and more elastic than coaxial cables. They cost about twenty-five cents per foot (forty cents if paired) and are getting cheaper. Figure 5.1 shows how fiber works.

Because the light signal is reflected (or "refracted") inward by changes in the cable's optical index of refraction, security is increased: the cables are hard to break into undetected. Their nonconducting "dielectric" properties isolate terminals electrically from each other, eliminating short circuit or shock hazards and grounding loops. Since they do not conduct current, they are safe even near explosives.

Figure 5.1 Basic fiber optic communications link.

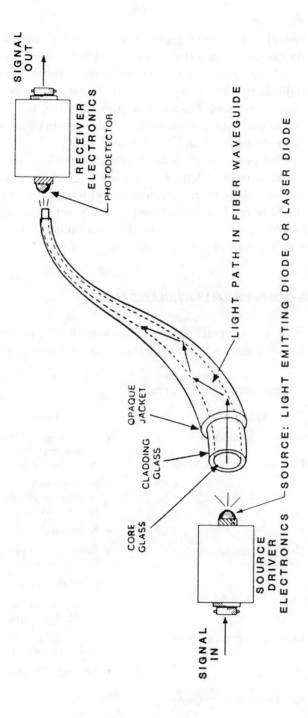

Channel (waveband) integrity is improved because the nonconducting fibers are unaffected by electromagnetic interference (EMI) from nearby power cables, factory machines, antennas, switches, or even lightning. Nor do they radiate signals that might interfere with the devices just listed. Optical fiber can be buried in the ground, installed in ducts (no poisonous PVC fires), wrapped around large objects, or strung overheard. See Figure 5.2.

The fiber optic unique portion of a LAN encompasses only the lowest OSI layer (see Chapter 1). It possesses little intelligence and does not contribute to the communication services provided by the higher OSI layers. In a general purpose LAN using microprocessor-based servers for the other layers, the fiber optic components may represent less than 10 percent of the cost.

SOME COMMERCIALLY AVAILABLE LANS

Today there are literally dozens of commercially available optical fiber LANS. Figure 5.3 lists a small fraction of them and should not

Figure 5.2 In general, why fiber optics?

Feature	Benefit
• Dielectric isolation	• No grounding, shock lightning problems
• EMI free (electromagnetic interference)	• No pickup of interference
	• Does not radiate electromagnetically (safety and interference)
	• No crosstalk problems
• Greater signal bandwidth for cable size	• Lower plant upgrade costs, facility modification
	• Better facility usage
	• Ability to combine signals (FDM, TDM Multiplex)
• Lower transmission losses	• Fewer repeaters (lower maintenance costs)
	• Less signal degradation

Figure 5.3 Some available optical LANs.

PRODUCT	Whispernet	ProNET	Fiberway	Codenet	U/B Net 1
MANUFACTURER	FiberCom	Proteon	Artel	Codenoll	FiberLAN
TOPOLOGY	Ring	Ring	Ring	Star	Star
ARBITRATION	CSMA/CD	Token	TimeShr	CSMA/CD	CSMA/CD
MAX SIZE	4 kmtrs	2.5 km	Open	1.5	1.8
MAX NODES	1024	255	32	1024	1024
BIT RATE	10 Mb/s	10/80	200	10	10
FIBER SIZE	.05/.125mm	.1/.14	.1/.14	.1/.14	.1/.14
FAULT TOLERANCE	Node byp, Dual ring	Node byp	Dual ring	Redundant Repeaters	None

necessarily be assumed to contain the best one for the reader's installation. Arbitration is explained in Chapter 1, and topology and fault tolerance are dealt with in some detail below.

WHICH TOPOLOGY FOR FIBER

Ring and star topologies (see Chapter 1) are advisable for fiber optic LANs, buses usually are not.

Optical tap couplers typically split half the available light at each node. Even without connector losses, by the fifth node the signal has dropped to one thirty-second of its original strength: $1/2 \times 1/2 \times 1/2 \times 1/2 \times 1/2 = 1/32$. The sixth and later modes of a bus would receive an even weaker signal.

In a passive optical fiber star network, light is sent from each transceiver over a two-fiber cable (one transmit fiber and one receive fiber) to a central "star coupler." The star divides the light more or less equally and sends a portion to each of the transceivers on the network. Thus a star coupler can support 32 nodes with a stronger signal than would have reached the sixth node on a passive fiber bus. See Figure 5.4.

In a fiber ring, each node is an active repeater. An incoming optical signal is converted to an electrical signal. This electrical signal is both tapped off to the node station and reconverted to an optical signal for retransmission to the next node. The station that originated the signal breaks the ring by "sinking" its own transmission.

Figure 5.4 A passive optical star.

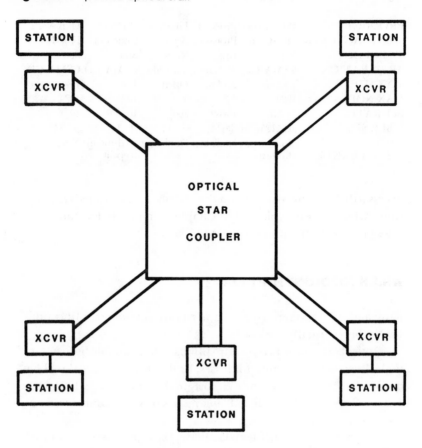

For a few dozen stations over limited distances, a passive star is recommended: There are no costly conversion mechanisms, no resulting node delays, and no network failure if one node dies and cannot pass the signal along.

An active ring is preferred in the opposite circumstances. If there are many stations, repeaters would have to be purchased to connect several passive stars together. If distances are large, cabling to the center could be costly. And ring expansion is convenient due to the simple path and the fact that the signal is renewed at each node.

Single-point failure on the ring can be handled by an optical

Figure 5.5 Counter rotating dual rings.

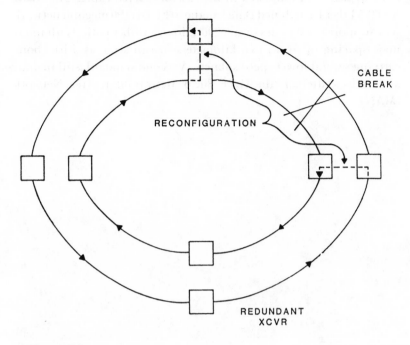

COUNTER ROTATING DUAL RINGS

equivalent of the node bypass discussed for rings in Chapter 1. In some fiber rings, however, the danger of either a failed station or a broken cable is taken care of by an entirely different solution—a second "backward" ring through which a redundant signal travels in the opposite direction. (See Figure 5.5).

In the case of a severed cable, the transceivers on either side of the break reach out to their twins so that one large ring is formed out of the remaining portions of the primary and redundant rings.

FUTURE STANDARDS

There are two related ongoing LAN standards activities involving dual counter-rotating fiber optic rings with active nodes, electrical node bypass, and loopback in the case of severed cable. The ANSI X3T9.5 Fiber Distributed Data Interface (FDDI) 100 megabit network will support 1,000 nodes over a 200-kilometer fiber path. With inter-node spacing of up to two kilometers, it can serve as a backbone carrying several lower speed subnets. A second standard, still in draft as this is written, is the IEEE 802.6 Metropolitan Area Network (MAN).

Peter Buttros
Corvus Systems, Inc.

6

Network Operating Systems and Security

An operating system is the set of management programs that decides what happens on the LAN and how it happens. There are many different types and levels of LAN operating systems. This chapter discusses operating systems for personal computer LANs and their security aspects. We will be looking at three categories of operating systems in order of increasing complexity: *disk service, file service, and total resource service.* See Figure 6.1.

Figure 6.1 Disk drives and other servers.

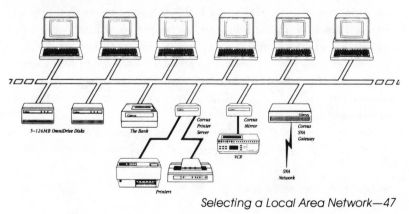

In disk service, the network's shield disk is divided into portions called partitions or volumes. Each volume is treated as if it were an internal hard disk on the corresponding machine, usually a PC. Communication between partitions is difficult since none of the PCs knows about the other.

In file service, the PC makes program calls to the file service software, which dynamically shrinks and expands disk space allocations.

DISK SERVICE

A disk-server-based system is the least complex (and least expensive) true network. Each user is allowed to share the resources of a common disk drive, but there is usually no facility in the operating system for file locking. This leaves the responsibility of file security to the designers of file handling software packages. These designers must customize their software products to work with each different LAN operating system. If they did not do this, several users could attempt to access a file at once with the danger of uncontrolled writing to that file.

This danger does not usually arise when individual users are creating files for their own use. For example, when using a word processing package, each user creates his or her own data file. Such files are automatically protected by the operating system because it allows only the owner of that file to have both READ and WRITE access to it.

Any other user on the LAN may be granted access to the file in question, but in a READ ONLY fashion. Such a restriction protects the data from being overwritten by people to whom it does not belong. This is the lowest level of security acceptable in a LAN.

The operating system may also allow for what are called "uncontrolled shared" areas. In that case, a multi-user software package, tailored for that LAN's operating system, can control its own file and record locking in that area.

Besides security, disk server operating systems allow for limited sharing of other resources on the network. They may allow dissimilar

Figure 6.2 Special area to merge unlike files.

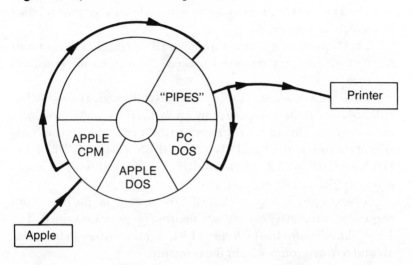

PCs to share the same resources. For example, Corvus Systems' Constellation II software permits IBM PCs, Apples, and some DEC computers to share TEXT files, printers and backup devices. To accomplish this the operating system sets up a special area on the disk drive known as a pipe partition, a sort of resting point for data. From the pipes area, the data may then proceed to a printer or other peripheral device. Or this may be used as a place for the merging of dissimilar files, such as a Macintosh Jazz file and an IBM PC's Lotus 1-2-3 file. See Figure 6.2.

In 1986, disk service was the only category of LAN operating system for Apple PCs because Apple had not yet issued standards for multi-user applications. By contrast, Microsoft's DOS 3.1 established file service as the standard for IBM compatible PC networks.

FILE SERVICE

The next more sophisticated (and costly) category of LAN operating system supplies individual file service, not just (physical) disk service. These LANs control file locking and thus permit several users to safely share the file server's disk drive without depending on a separate word processing program for security. Novell's Netware product is a widely used example.

A LAN operating system supplying file service has at least four levels of security: user/password, trustee/directory, group rights, and file flags.

A user is given access to the network server through a password but still needs the right to reference any given directory (set of programs) on that server. The rights "entrusted" to the user can be any combination of the commands READ, WRITE, OPEN, CREATE, DELETE, OWNERSHIP, SEARCH, or MODIFY. These rights allow a user access to files as well as directories.

For example, a directory called "Wordproc" might have word processing, dictionary editing, and mailing programs as subsets. The LAN administrator has to decide which rights to assign to individuals and to user groups within the company.

Different groups have different directory rights for the example given. Secretaries would certainly need to be entrusted with nearly all the rights listed earlier. But billing clerks might only be granted READ, OPEN, and SEARCH so that they would be able to examine the contents of a file but not modify it. The LAN administrator would be still more selective with most groups when issuing rights to a confidential file.

The final level of security mentioned above is that of file flags. File flags can be set by each file's owner to permit access by READ/WRITE SHARING, READ ONLY SHARING, or READ ONLY NONSHAREABLE. See Figure 6.3.

FASTER FILE SERVICE ACCESS

Security is only one of the functions of a LAN operating system. It can speed up the process of information sharing through such features as directory hashing, directory caching, file caching, and elevator seeking. See Figure 6.4.

Directory hashing is a process where the operating system creates and retains sorted indexes of the disk file locations so the directories

Figure 6.3 File flags.

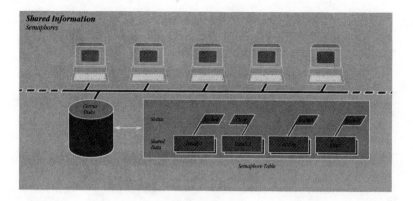

are found faster. This can save as much as 30 percent of the time spent by sequential searches for the disk files themselves.

In directory caching, "file allocation tables" (FATs) are stored in core memory itself, so that the directories are written and read directly from core, thus eliminating disk bottlenecks where many reads are involved. This technique alone can reduce access time by as much as 99 percent.

In file caching, the entire file is stored in core so that the files are referenced directly instead of going to the disk for each read or write. Of course file caching is limited by core memory size, but the operating system also controls this by "swapping in" the frequently used files and "swapping out" files that are not being used much at that time.

Separately, elevator seeking makes reading from (or writing to) the disk drive a more efficient physical process. Ordinarily, requests for the drive would be processed on a first-come, first-served basis. But with elevator seeking, requests are reorganized into the order that is most efficient for that drive. Figure 6.5 shows four requests that have been resequenced so that they will be fulfilled smoothly as the disk drive arm moves inward along the disk surface. Elevator seeking can reduce physical disk access time by as much as 40 percent. See Figure 6.5.

Figure 6.4 Time-consuming disk indexing, seek, and rotation.

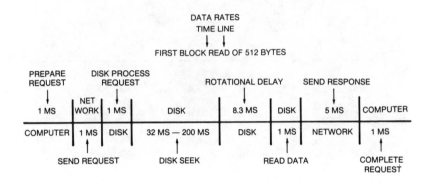

TOTAL RESOURCE SERVICE

A new generation of LAN operating systems aims at making the existence of the network transparent to the user. He or she logs onto the network using an ID and password, but then uses only the regular PC commands (PC/DOS, for example), not network commands.

With this total resource service, the user has access to a "search and connect" utility. It allows the user to browse around the network and make connections to any of the network resources desired. Since the LAN operating system now enables access to any network resource (nodes, drives, peripherals, directories), it is necessary to have a reliable security system that restricts a user to particular resources.

A total resource operating system provides separate access control for nodes on the network, the peripherals on each node, directories and files. The security is based on an extensive "access control list" rather than on password protection of directories as is found in File Service operating systems.

Access here is controlled by specifying the "privilege level" (1 to 100) that a user (or group) must have to examine or update the

Figure 6.5 Elevator seeking.

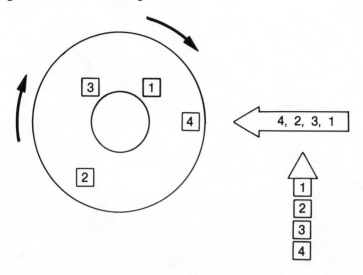

resource. All users that attempt to access the resource have their privileges compared to the access levels specified by the owner of the resource.

As in the file service level of operating systems, total resource must also provide support for multi-user program packages. This is done by using file and record locks both for multiple use of single-user software and for multi-user software. In order to be in the high performance range, it also facilitates all of the hashing and caching and elevator seeking techniques explained earlier.

Some aspects of "total resource" are already available in existing products. Others are only in the announcement phase and can best be described as "vaporware." Most readers with IBM compatible PCs will probably best be served by a LAN than can communicate with DOS version 3.1 or a later DOS version (such as 5.0).

Cheryl Snapp
Novell, Inc.

7

Bridges between Local Area Networks

A bridge receives packets of information from one LAN and reassembles (or simply copies) them into packets of the format that a second LAN can accept, allowing information to pass freely from one network to the other. The bridge depicted in Figure 7.1 consists of software residing on a host device.

Network bridges are the links that enable the various LANs to speak to each other. This internetworking, or bridging, allows a particular file server or workstation to connect like and unlike LAN topologies or physical media so that all users can communicate with each other and gain access to all file servers. This category is also expanding to include remote LAN-to-LAN communications. See Figure 7.1.

Figure 7.1 LAN A packets converted for LAN B.

(   )——(   )——(   )——[network bridge]——(   )——(   )——(   )—
LAN A   Information   LAN B   Information
            packets   packets

A bridge can be implemented either "internally," within a network file server, or "externally," through an individual workstation. An external workstation need not be dedicated for use only as a bridge. However there are sound reasons to install the bridge either within the file server or in a dedicated personal computer used only for this purpose, thus protecting the speed and functionality of the bridge.

If users are performing other applications on a bridge workstation, their throughput can slow down considerably during periods of heavy bridge workload. But if dedicated only to interconnectivity, the bridge workstation always has access to enough memory to operate at its maximum level without interfering with the users' program performance. Even more important, if the bridge resides on a nondedicated user station and the user needs to reboot (restart) that station, the entire bridge may be in jeopardy.

In addition to the bridging software itself, a bridge must include a network interface card corresponding to each LAN being bridged. The cards may be placed wherever there is physical capacity. Placement within the bridge workstation is illustrated in Figure 7.2.

BRIDGE APPLICATIONS

The main function of a bridge is to allow interconnection of multiple LANs. One may be tempted to think in terms of bridging only LANs of unlike topology, allowing different types to operate out of the same file server. This is, however, only one of four broad areas of application.

- *Is growth inhibited?* A user with a LAN that can no longer be expanded (maximum nodes or obsolete hardware), or who desires to incorporate a new LAN with greater capabilities, can bridge the old and new networks together. This saves the investment in the original equipment.
- *Is the LAN overloaded?* One large expanding LAN can be broken into two or more LANs to increase processing speed and to decrease cabling costs. For example, Figure 7.4 illustrates

Figure 7.2 Bridge between similar LANs.

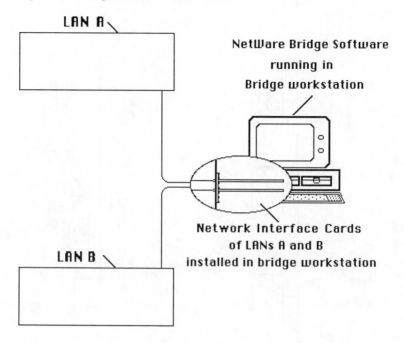

what began as one large network shared by the accounting and manufacturing departments. Because of slow speeds and the cabling costs necessary to add more user stations, the decision has been made to split the two groups. All users can still communicate as though they were on one LAN, but now have the speed and operational flexibility of two smaller LANs. See Figure 7.3.

• *Are distances too great?* Bridging can circumvent distance limitations. A network that could originally span 4,000 feet can now expand to 8,000 feet if the configuration is broken into two separate networks joined by a bridge in the file server. The conversion of one LAN in Figure 7.3 to two LANs in Figure 7.4 has another desirable outcome: Bandwidth (Mb/s) available to

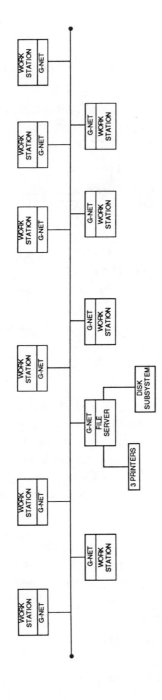

Figure 7.3 Original LAN before splitting.

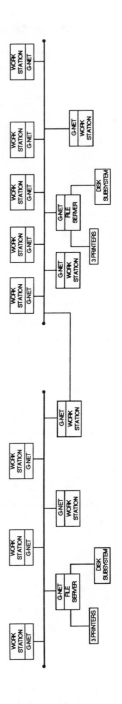

Figure 7.4 Two LANs accommodate more.

the workstations effectively increases, boosting file server efficiency at the cost of a single network interface card.

- *Should two LANs join together?* Several historically distinct LANs can be interconnected. Suppose a firm has had different LANs serving different departments but they must now share and utilize information previously not available to them. Depending on the capacity of the operating system, some of the file servers may become unnecessary or could be better used elsewhere. This is shown in Figure 7.5 for LANs which have compatible frames (packets). However, in the general case a device called a gateway is needed for distinctly different LAN products, and the reader is referred to Chapter 8 for further discussion.

Figure 7.5 Bridging LANs together.

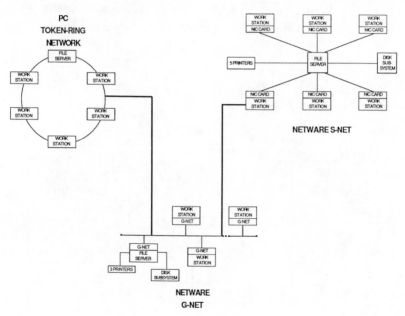

WHAT THE BRIDGE DOES

In generic terms, a bridge (sometimes called a data link relay) is a node-level passageway for the lower layers of a protocol. Under the OSI model (see Chapter 1), these sub-network layers are the lowest three: Network, Data Link and Physical. In terms of this book, a bridge handles internetworking at Layer 2, and a gateway does this job instead if Layer 3 is involved.

The packets entering a bridge include addresses of nodes along the LANs it connects. Thus a bridge must have routing intelligence, or at least needs to know which addresses belong to the networks to which it is directly connected.

Figure 7.6 illustrates in general terms how a bridge or gateway fits the OSI model. Suppose a common set of packet headers and trailers exists for workstation-to-workstation communication within a network. (In Novell products, this inner frame of the full packet is named IPX, intranetwork packet exchange.) If the overall packet is to go from an Ethernet LAN to an ARCNET LAN, the outer shells of the packet must be stripped off and replaced, as shown in Figure 7.7.

Figure 7.6 Bottom three OSI layers.

LAN A	BRIDGE	LAN B
Application		Application
Presentation		Presentation
Session		Session
Transport		Transport
Network		Network
Link		Link
Physical		Physical

The Data Link component (Layer 2) strips off the Ethernet header and Ethernet trailer and hands the inner frame to the Network layer. The Network component examines the IPX frame and decides which new header and trailer are required and what size packet is necessary to enter the receiving LAN. Network (Layer 3) then hands the packet (with instructions) back to Data Link (Layer 2) to have it refurbished with an ARCNET header and trailer. The packet can now be sent out as a chain of bits by Layer 1 (Physical) and travel along the receiving LAN, successfully reaching the desired destination.

In a bridge, although the directions come from Layer 3, Network, the actual dissection and encapsulation of the packets takes place at Layer 2, Data Link. There are cases where Layer 3 must do more work, for example, connection to an external computer or a wide area network (WAN). The devices that do this strictly "external" connection are known as gateways and are discussed in Chapter 8.

Figure 7.7 Converting frames.

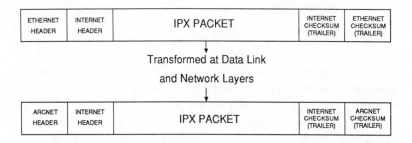

Efrem Goldberg
Carolyn Guzy
Bridge Communications, Inc.

8

Gateways and Common Carriers

There are very few exclusively *local* local area networks. Considerations of LAN size, distance, media type, and other unavoidable differences among networks will not go away.

In the past, remote access to applications was provided on a case-by-case basis by special purpose, not general purpose, networks. The telecommunications software for any of these networks was application dependent.

Today, the spanning of different protocols, as necessary as the spanning of distances, is implemented through devices known as bridges, routers, and gateways.

BRIDGES, ROUTERS, AND GATEWAYS

As discussed in Chapter 7, bridges can increase the number of addressable nodes or link two geographically distinct LANs—without signing on to a communications service, dialing through a modem, or learning new software commands. Gateways translate one network protocol to another, surmounting both hardware and software incompatibility. Routers provide alternate communication paths to ensure high data transfer and reliable transmission.

In the general case, key hardware or software resources may already have been optimized for particular applications. They are located geographically at a place where they are most easily maintained or most intensively used. And their different requirements have led to different network technologies.

OSI AND OTHER STANDARDS

The matrix in Figure 8.1 illustrates the relationship among the most widely accepted network standards, both official and de facto. Most of these standards are covered in detail in Chapter 1 or subsequent chapters.

Along the horizontal axis are the low-level protocols comprising OSI Layer 1 (Physical) and Layer 2 (Data Link). The vertical axis contains single entries for OSI and non-OSI network standards for the functions in which they correspond to OSI Layers 3 through 7. (Shaded areas correspond to bridge communications products available as of this writing.)

The eighteen intersection boxes of Figure 8.1 constitute a minimum subset of all the possible protocols that a network implementer must be prepared to cope with.

BRIDGES AT ISO LAYERS 1 AND 2

Internetwork devices are referred to as bridges, routers, or gateways, depending on the OSI layers they touch. Bridges and routers require a protocol match between at least one corresponding pair of ISO layers. Bridges require a match at OSI Layer 2 (Data Link, as shown in Chapter 7) or even at Layer 1. Routers need only a match at Layer 3 (Network). By contrast, gateways can perform a full protocol conversion and might not demand a match at any layer.

Bridges are the most general of internetwork devices because they operate at the lowest two levels of the OSI hierarchy. They "don't care" about any higher level functions. Therefore, traffic for several different higher level protocols can be passed through the same bridge.

Layer 1 bridges function by passing signals between two different physical media, such as a token bus and a CSMA bus.

There are two types of Layer 2 bridges. One type connects two LANs running the same operating system (see Chapter 6) and separated for strategic reasons only (longer distance or more nodes). The other type (sometimes called "two half bridges") joins two LANs that are separated by an intermediate network such as a point-to-point telephone circuit.

Layer 2 bridges are further divided into "dumb" and "smart" bridges. Passive (dumb) bridges pass all traffic on one network over to the other. Smart ("protocol independent") bridges send only traffic explicitly directed to the other network, searching each frame to find the destination address and then comparing it to a network address table. Because the process of media access control (MAC) is a subset of Layer 2, smart bridges are also referred to as MAC level bridges.

Figure 8.1 Table of protocols.

STANDARDS AND MARKETS

High Level Protocols

	IEEE 802.3 Ethernet	IEEE 802.4 Token Bus	IEEE 802.5 Token Ring
DECNET	DEC Installed Base		
X.25	Gateway to X.25		
SNA	Gateway to SNA		IBM Installed Base
ISO	International TOP	Factory Automation	
TCP/IP	UNIX CAE/CAD DoD		
XNS	Office Automation		

Low Level Protocols

ROUTERS AT OSI LAYER 3

Routers, like MAC level bridges, selectively pass packets between networks. But they are "protocol dependent," acting specifically only on packets which observe one particular higher level protocol. Layer 2 address headers and trailers are ignored because they represent individual devices on a network. But Layer 3 address information is used because it identifies which network houses that device.

Interestingly, for any given set of protocols in Figure 1, only Layer 3 contains any reference to individual networks. If a protocol set has no Network Layer headers or trailers, it only "sees" one large network. Thus in large multi-site organizations the scope of such networks is limited.

Many PC network products are designed without a Network Layer to reduce their complexity and program size. This omission may cause serious inconvenience and complication once the network grows beyond the original limited workgroup whose needs it used to serve nicely.

A router operates by accepting packets from one LAN that are addressed to another. It inspects the Layer 3 address and decides which LAN must receive the packet. In the simplest case, the router may have only one attached network and this decision is trivial. But in multi-line the decision is more complicated, and the router may have to be a powerful computer in its own right.

MAC level bridges cannot function properly when there is more than one route to any other network. Yet in very large networks, multiple routes are required to minimize route length. In Figure 8.2, a

Figure 8.2 Need for a router.

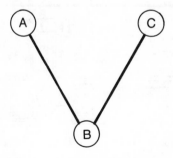

packet must pass through node B to go from A to C. A router would enable a connection from A to C directly, eliminating the extra trip through B.

Clearly, any valid Layer 3 protocol will allow the router to know the status of the various routes available. Sometimes the corresponding procedures are included in higher OSI layers, but they must always be present.

GATEWAYS TO WANS AND MAINFRAMES

Gateways are used to permit communication between systems running different protocols. They can be used to link different LANs, but they are most effective in linking LANs to wide area networks or to local mainframes that use the WAN protocols. Both situations are illustrated in Figure 8.3 and explained below.

Circuit ("hard wired") switching was the original signal routing

Figure 8.3 Bridge's GS/1 gateway connecting LAN and WAN.

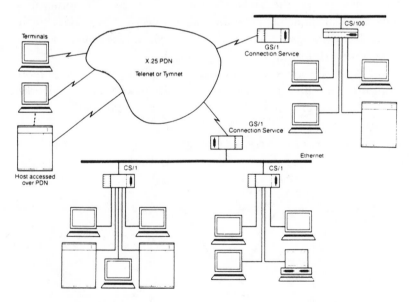

technique used in the telephone system, and it is still present today in local voice systems. When a voice call is made a unique physical path is set up through the telephone network for the duration of the call. When a data line is set up (dial-up or leased), it also occupies a specific path through the telephone network.

During a typical data call, the line is idle most of the time. The user is either reading the latest output, thinking about it, or typing at a very low speed. Still, that call is tying up a circuit.

"Packet switching" reclaims that idle time by mixing the traffic of many users over the same line. The data streams of the individual users are assembled into packets (frames) like those in LANs and passed around by addresses in "virtual" (not hard wired) circuits, again like those in LANs. The short dashed line at the left of Figure 8.3 is an example of a virtual circuit. In the abstract, such WANs are very similar to LANs in the way they transfer data.

CCCIT's X.25 specification is by far the most popular WAN protocol. It is the basis for GTE Telenet, Tymnet, other public packet switching services, and many private WANs as well. X.25 has been designed specifically for wide area communications on today's telephone company lines, where many alternate paths usually are available between any two points.

All X.25 Public Data Networks (PDNs) offer a choice among data rates of 2.4 KB/s, 4.8 Kb/s and 9.6 Kb/s. Addresses consist of three digits for country, plus one for the PDN's own ID, and up to ten additional digits to identify the device on that PDN. Each X.25 packet can convey up to 128 bytes of data.

Protocol conversion from Ethernet to X.25 is illustrated in Figure 8.4. A LAN-to-X.25 gateway can permit a user on the LAN to communicate with a user or host on the X.25 network: a user connected to the X.25 network to call a host on the LAN, or a host on the LAN to communicate with a host on the X.25 network. The long dashed lines in Figure 8.5 illustrate the four classes of gatewayed virtual circuits.

When a user initiates a call that crosses from a LAN to an X.25 net, the gateway takes the virtual circuit from the LAN and connects it to a virtual circuit on the X.25 net. Once the call is set up, the gateway translates the LAN packets to the other format and maps the LAN

Figure 8.4 Converting an 802.3 packet to an X.25 packet.

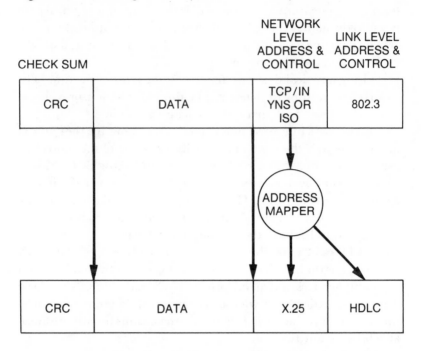

address to the X.25 destination address. The packet net takes over from there.

As a second example, Systems Network Architecture (SNA) is IBM's principal WAN protocol. Well defined and stable, it is an effective way for LANs to access IBM host computers. Consider an Ethernet to SNA gateway that lets a collection of devices or PCs on a LAN look instead (to the IBM mainframe) like a grouping of IBM 3278 terminals. Using the gateway instead of individual emulator cards can save not only on the integrated cards but also on cabling cost that would have to be incurred in connecting each node directly to the mainframe.

PERFORMANCE CONSIDERATIONS

Any internetwork server is a shared network resource, much the same as a file or print server, but busier.

Figure 8.5 Four LAN/WAN virtual circuits.

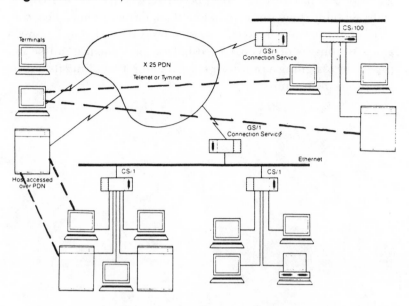

A gateway receives and processes many more packets than other network stations and must exhibit higher performance and reliability. At Layer 6, it may be constantly translating between ASCII format data on one side and EBCDIC format on the other. At Layer 5, it must initiate, answer, monitor and terminate sessions, all the while keeping the existence of the second network (and itself) transparent to the business users.

Consider, too, the substantial computing power and temporary ("buffer") storage needed to handle either bursts or steady streams of incoming or outgoing traffic:

- to receive arbitrarily long sequences of back-to-back packets, each of arbitrary size
- to buffer large amounts of incoming data for subsequent processing by a LAN server or CPU on either side
- to report multiple events to these processes without generating large overhead.

From a hardware standpoint, it is fairly easy to replace or augment a gateway that has, through time, been overwhelmed by traffic. If it addresses more than one external network or mainframe, these contacts might be split between two or more gateways. Or, because a gateway consists of two balanced halves, performance can be improved by assigning a processor to each half for handling its respective protocol structure.

Kathryn A. Petry
Pamela E. Valentine
3Com Corp

Alan W. Laster
Richard G. Lefkon
Citicorp, N.A.

Charles J. Letizia
Lance S. Sprung
Wang Laboratories, Inc.

9

Automated Office: Mail, Files, Voice, and Image

This chapter introduces some of the specific electronic procedures in the office. It covers electronic mail, switching of voice and data, and IBM-oriented protocols in some depth. Chapter 12, on the TOP protocols project, discusses the effort to standardize office LANs.

THE FOUR MOST BASIC LAN SERVICES

Large or small, LANs nearly always provide these four network-based services: print service, mail service, file service, and access elsewhere.

A shared desktop laser printer is silent and can produce thousands of originals per day. If it is busy, it will queue arriving print jobs until it is free. The user can go on working without waiting for printing to end.

Electronic mail is sent from a user who is logged on to one who might not be. By specifying distribution lists, a single message can reach an entire group (such as the regional sales managers) without the need to key in every name. A mail recipient can forward (or return) the incoming message with an attached reply, print it, delete it, or save it indefinitely.

Multi-user file service may involve such commands as SHARE (create a shared file), SHUTDOWN (disallow its use), MOD (change its password, etc.), UNSHARE, and HELP (always a plus). File servers can govern a mixture of private, public (write-protected) and shared resources, as discussed in Chapter 6. Network security, examined in the same chapter, becomes increasingly important as LAN use is integrated into important business functions. Security (and remote access) can be made more effective by selecting a network which supports permanent, unique names for users and resources; as of this writing, IBM LANs do not.

Access outside the LAN may consist of a bridge to another LAN (Chapter 7) or a gateway to a dissimilar network or a mainframe computer (Chapter 8). See Figure 9.1.

OSI LAYER 7 FOR OFFICE APPLICATIONS

Layering is the basic structure used in the OSI model explained in Chapter 1. Each system is composed of a set of subsystems with logically related functions.

As far as the end user is concerned, the application layer is perhaps the most important, for it is the final layer between technology and human interaction. File transfer commands, electronic mail and voice messaging systems are good examples of applications within a distributed network.

Figure 9.1 3 Com's LAN gateway to SNA.

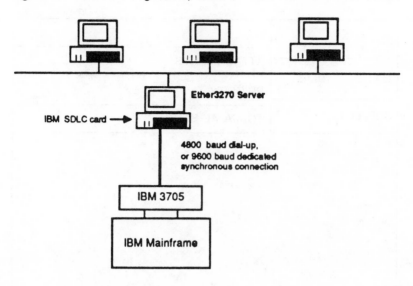

SENDING ELECTRONIC MAIL

Many essentially equivalent electronic mail software packages are available for LAN use. A good mail system will incorporate screen formats that allow for composing, storing, printing, editing and forwarding.

Upon invoking the mail function, a user receives a main mail menu screen similar to the one shown in Figure 9.2. This format allows entry of message information in a preformatted way.

The upper left portion of the screen provides input fields for the standard memorandum heading information; only topic needs to be input, the rest are linked to the logon ID or the system clock. On the right are input fields for the addressee(s) and for concluding notations, such as a carbon copy list, which (on a manually typed letter) would be entered at the end.

Figure 9.2 Main mail menu.

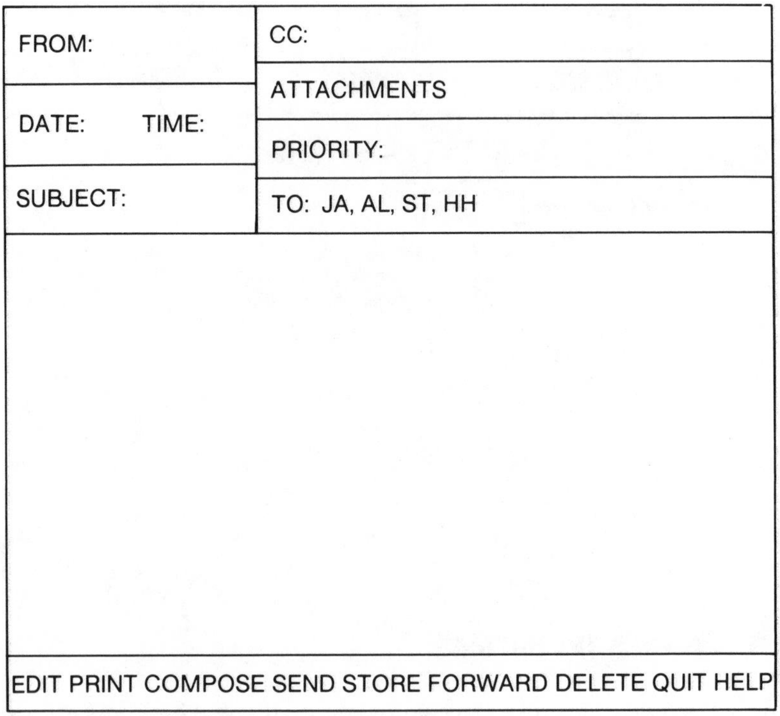

FROM:	CC:	
DATE: TIME:	ATTACHMENTS	
	PRIORITY:	
SUBJECT:	TO: JA, AL, ST, HH	
EDIT PRINT COMPOSE SEND STORE FORWARD DELETE QUIT HELP		

The center of the screen serves as a word processor to receive the actual mail text. The bottom offers cursor-selected functions such as COMPOSE and SEND. After selecting the COMPOSE function, the user enters identifying information in the appropriate fields, filling the addressee and carbon copy fields with two-letter abbreviations for individuals or mailing lists known to the mail system.

The memo text is composed in nearly the same way it would be on a typewriter; for instance, the ENTER key is used to skip lines. A special DELETE key eliminates all text to the right of the cursor, while an INSERT key permits adding text between words. When the memo is completed, the user presses the ESC(ape) key and regains the display of selectable functions at the bottom of the screen.

Selecting the STORE and SEND functions accomplishes those tasks.

The recipient receives a musical tone and the screen shown in Figure 9.3, either immediately (if logged on) or upon next entering the system.

The Mail Received or Stored screen presents a table of files for that user. To read a piece of mail, the user moves the cursor to the desired SUBJECT and presses ENTER, producing a memorandum image on the screen.

To modify a stored mail file, the user selects the EDIT function from the basic screen in Figure 9.3 and then chooses the subject from the Mail Received or Stored.

FILE TRANSFER ON A PC LAN

File access and security are covered extensively in Chapter 6. The act of sending an entire file is different from reading or writing to a file

Figure 9.3 Available mail list.

MAIL RECEIVED OR STORED

FROM	DATE	TIME	SUBJECT
READ		DELETE	QUIT HELP

elsewhere on a LAN. The file may be small, as it often is for electronic mail. It may, however, be large.

The most popular protocol for asynchronous file transmission is known as XMODEM. It is used in the file transfer software of many currently available PC communication software packages. XMODEM replaces the parity check bit in the simpler asychronous frames (see Figure 1.4) with a numeric "checksum" byte. This byte is computed as the total of the binary number equivalents for all bytes (as many as 128) in the message, divided by 255. The resulting frame is shown in Figure 9.4.

Although the packet itself is larger and more intelligent than a single byte transmission, XMODEM is still an asynchronous protocol: an ACK or NAK must be received before the next transmission.

Two less-established asynchronous protocols for file transmission are BLAST and X.PC. As implied by its name, X.PC is an asynchronous version of X.25 (see Chapter 8); it is used by Tymnet. BLocked ASynchronous Transmission has frames that resemble those for SDLC shown in Figure 1.4.

FILE TRANSFER WITH AN IBM MAINFRAME

The least decentralized synchronous office protocol has now added peer connectivity.

In adding a theoretical object called a PU (Physical Unit) 2.1, IBM's SNA (see Chapter 8) for the first time stepped out of its mainframe-centered world.

Previously, a LAN gateway was seen on the other side by SNA as a peripheral device subordinate to the central computer. Nodes along the LAN were not recognized as independent entities, only as internal

Figure 9.4 XMODEM protocol asynchronous frame.

START BYTE	BLOCK SEQUENCE NUMBER	ADDL. SEQUENCE NUMBER	DATA up to 128 BYTES DATA	CHECKSUM BYTE

features of the gateway. By instituting PU 2.1, SNA may not have become quite so sharing as the LAN example described in Chapter 10, but it has moved somewhat closer. Now a device on an SNA WAN can communicate directly with an equivalent device without being censored by the mainframe at the hub.

Once the device on the node has been defined as a PU 2.1 (or something else), the actual software which sets up the data transfer will need an IBM classification as well. SNA's LU (Logical Unit) 6.2 is a classification applied to the particular application program which is communicating with the network.

An LU 6.2 program must exchange information using a particular set of verb meanings, such as SEND-DATA and RECEIVE-AND-WAIT. The LU 6.2 classification for programs can apply not only to those residing on LAN devices but to programs on centralized IBM applications (such as "CICS" and "DB II" software) as well.

DISOSS: IBM ELECTRONIC MAIL

The LU 6.2 Layer 7 protocol just described can also be used in sending electronic mail between word processors that work differently from each other. IBM's Distributed Office Support System (DISOSS) is a special set of application software that classifies a transmitted document into one of three formats: final, mixed final (text plus graphics) and revisable. Add-ons and forwarding by the recipient, as described earlier, have certain limitations in DISOSS. A new industry-wide standard, CCITT's X.400, has now been adopted for TOP and is being pursued by other electronic mail vendors as well.

THE X.400 STANDARD

An X.400 message handling system (MHS) is said to transfer an envelope accompanying content, in analogy with a frame's protocol information and data. The content portion can consist either of a free-form report or a heading-and-body combination somewhat like that in Figure 9.2.

The user's OSI Layer 7 (Application) contact point within the MHS is referred to as a user agent (UA). X.400 divides Layer 7 into two sublayers, one each for actions of this user agent and the MHS's so-called transfer agent.

The Layer 6 (Presentation) encoding unit, called a data element, contains prefix information as to its type and length, followed by the message data itself. The classification and enumeration of data elements is more involved than the descriptions of frames given in Chapters 1, 7, and 8.

By grouping data elements, an X.400 message can mix text, graphics, and digitized audio and image data.

PBX FOR VOICE AND DATA

Businesses have traditionally used twisted pair networks for telephone service and coaxial cable networks for access to computers. Digital private branch exchanges can combine voice and data on the same facilities wherever users do not require sustained high data throughput.

Voice and data calls are handled identically by a typical PBX, shown schematically in Figure 9.5. Such devices are not true LANs, as communication is centralized, not distributed. But since LANs can dial them up over a WAN, it may be useful to have a general idea of how PBX programming operates.

The user at the workstation picks up the telephone, and user interface (bottom center) notifies Control (upper left) of this. Control asks the user for the desired extension. Then user interface collects and verifies the digits and tells Switching (lower left), which verifies validity of the number. User Interface rings the recipient phone and caller headset, and stops the ringing when the phone is picked up.

The result in real life is that, once the button is pressed on workstation A, the telephone at workstation B rings and the print server at node C produces the document.

Figure 9.5 Functional view of Wang/Telenova PBX.

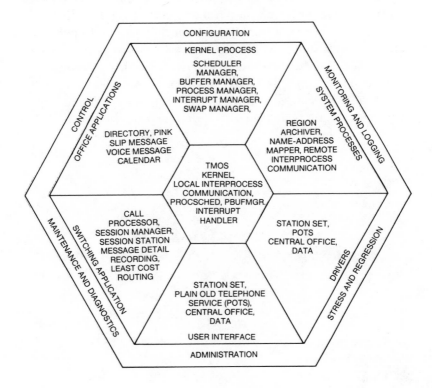

DIGITIZED VOICE AND IMAGE

Digital voice store and forward messaging and voice response can piggy-back onto existing office automation systems. Typically these require 10,000 to 50,000 bits per second to digitize the sound. Some storage systems permit the stored files to be edited from and reassembled, much like splicing a recording tape.

Similarly, images need a great deal of storage if they are digitized rather than deciphered by an optical scanner. Inexpensive scanners that can read in a page of typed mail in several seconds are now available. These scanners recognize one of a dozen standard print fonts and store the printed or typed text in a standard PC file.

Whether by optical scanning or image digitizing, the two procedures just mentioned go a long way toward producing a truly "paperless" office: they help the user throw away paper that already exists, not just force future recordkeeping to occur on a terminal or PC. LANs also are currently available which present a divided screen which both displays an image of the original paper and provides a full 3278-format input area.

John Adams
Digital Equipment Corp.

10

You Don't Have to Fire the Mainframe

In the standard mainframe or minicomputer environment, a powerful central processing unit (CPU) sits at the logical center of things and controls all disk packs and terminals and printers as "peripheral" extensions of itself. If the system runs out of disk space, more disks are added; and if more terminals or communications are desired, terminals or communications are added.

This centralization contrasts sharply with the underlying connectivity (see Chapter 1) of a LAN, where all entities can communicate directly with each other at any time. Perhaps the most important aspect of such a system is the degree of resource sharing that is possible. Crucial data can be managed systematically but still remain available to anyone connected to the network. Printers in any location can be used by any system in the network to provide hard copy where it is geographically needed.

THREE MODES OF PROCESSING

This chapter discusses what the LAN concept means to mainframe processing in terms of three basic types of processing: interactive systems, background processing, and specialized services.

Interactive computing is needed to provide rapid response to the user, and hence it should be located as close to the user as possible. In most cases, this will cause the user to have his or her own personal computing resource in the form of a PC or workstation. Background computing is needed to do the processing tasks that are not interactive in nature, either because they are not time critical, or because the computing power required cannot be economically supplied on a personal level. Specialized computing is required for support of specific functions such as storing and retrieving files, printing, and communications.

In conjunction to mainframes, LANs cause these three types of computing to evolve: personal computing, in the form of PCs or workstations; background computing, in the form of compute servers; and specialized computing, in the form of servers dedicated to specific functions. This outcome is by no means obvious if one starts with the centralized case.

A PROGRESSION FROM CENTRALIZATION

Today, most office automation systems are timesharing systems that support multiple terminals. Either there is one CPU, or the terminals are connected into several computers through some kind of circuit switch such as a PBX or data switch. Thus the computing environment appears as shown in Figure 10.1.

A major difficulty with this system is the problem of the central switch blocking access for some of the users. As an example, if all the ports (mainframe entry points) from the switch to System A are in use, the next user who wants to use System A is blocked from accessing it until a port is freed up. Unfortunately, a very common behavior in office automation systems is for users to stay connected to their system for the entire day. Thus the network manager must either "over con-

Figure 10.1 Centralized timesharing on mainframe.

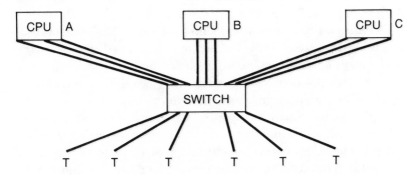

figure" the switch, which is very expensive, or accept the blocking problem, which is frequently unacceptable to the user.

Since a LAN works by time-division switching among packets (see Chapter 1) and not by switching entire circuits, many office automation users are solving the blocking problem by using a LAN. If the circuit switch is replaced by a LAN with one or more terminal servers, full connectivity results, as shown in Figure 10.2.

In this configuration, all the terminals in the network can connect to any computer in the network without being blocked, since the high speed links that attach the computers to the network can support a large number of simultaneous sessions. Thus, the LAN makes it possible to build a significantly more responsive automated office than would otherwise be possible. Except for the communication corridor, this is still a traditional timesharing environment.

If PCs are added to the LAN, a significantly different environment

Figure 10.2 Freer flow when LAN replaces switch.

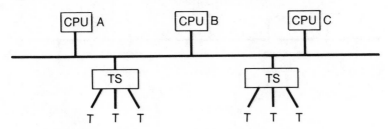

evolves, which may be called a distributed computing environment. This is shown in Figure 10.3.

At this point, the automation model changes. The more interactive processing moves to the PC, and the mainframe "servers" do the back-end processing functions that are less time-critical. Thus functions such as document preparation and modification, spreadsheet creation, and mail origination and termination will occur on the PCs. Functions such as document storage and retrieval, data storage and retrieval, and mail store and forward will occur on the mainframes. This hybrid environment has some of its processing done using the centralized timesharing model and the remainder done using a distributed computing model. Because of the individual hard PC disks, the distributed approach costs more, but it provides better performance.

Substituting a file server for the PC hard disks modifies the diagram only slightly, producing Figure 10.4. But now the network has

Figure 10.3 PC's, workstations add distributed processing.

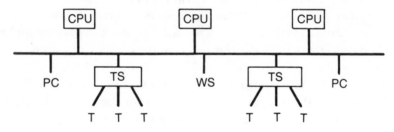

Figure 10.4 File server completes the transformation.

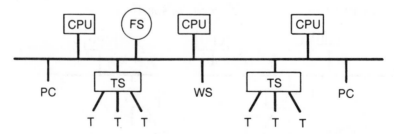

all three kinds of computing: the PCs are doing personal computing (document processing), the larger computers are doing background processing (document store and forward), and the file server and terminal servers are doing specialized processing.

The role of the mainframe has changed significantly: at the beginning, the computer was the system, but now the network itself is the system, and the general purpose computer has become just another peripheral device in the total office automation system.

Kevin Hughes
Allen-Bradley

11

MAP Protocols and the Factory

In 1981, General Motors set up a task force to study the effects of conflicting communication protocols on its computers (many manufactured by IBM, DEC, and Motorola), robots (GMF, Millacron), and programmable controllers (Gould, Square D, and Allen-Bradley). GM found that half the cost of automating new and retooled factories could be tied to communications supporting multiple proprietary networks. In some facilities, six or more communications wiring schemes occurred in parallel to meet different cable and protocol requirements.

In the interests of standardization, GM founded a 21-company project to produce a common Manufacturing Automation Protocol (MAP). This group today has over 200 member corporations. The protocols themselves were shaped to fit definitions by ANSI, EIA, IEEE and NBS. A key MAP aim was that off-the-shelf products from different vendors be able to interconnect and intercommunicate. See Figure 11.1.

Here the OSI layers of functional segmentation found their most

Figure 11.1 Evolution of the MAP effort.

Evolution of the MAP Effort

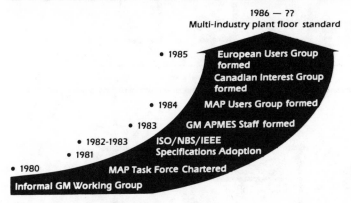

systematic application. As fixed protocols were given to particular layers, vendors could implement immediately the functionalities specified.

MAP AND OSI

MAP particularizes OSI Layer 7 with a standardized File Transfer Access Method (FTAM), Manufacturing Message Format Standard (MMFS) for programmable devices, and Common Application Service Elements (CASE) for interfacing with lower layers. It uses these communication protocols as specified by the MAP working committees and the International Standards Organization, as well as similar ones for Layers 5, 4 and 3.

Layers 2 and 1 are pinned down by the adoption of IEEE 802.4. Token bus is considered the best choice for manufacturing due to its deterministic, robust characteristics. Signals can be conveyed either by broadband or by what is known as carrier band. See Figure 11.2.

MAP installations use a broadband backbone and have many

Figure 11.2 Broadband and carrier band.

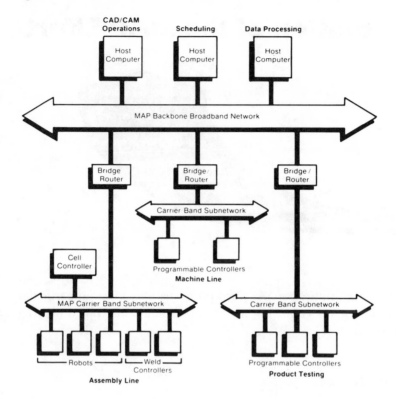

"factory cell" subnetworks, as shown in Figure 11.2. Programmable controllers and other node level devices attach to the subnetworks, not the backbone.

Like IEEE 802.4 broadband (see Chapter 4), the token passing carrier band uses coaxial cable to block out noise and appends its data to a "carrier" (analog) frequency. But like baseband (see Chapter 3), it occupies the entire cable for one network and is used primarily for sending binary data. Its 5 Mb/s throughput, although only half some Ethernet rates, provides fast response times over the short distances characteristic of factory cells.

A FACTORY EXAMPLE

Two well-known MAP applications are in Detroit automobile assembly plants. One is a new facility and the other a plant retrofit. In each case, the LANs interconnect a programmable device support system (PDSS), a manufacturing information database (MIDB) and approximately eighty robot controllers. See Figure 11.3.

The PDSS, based on a DEC VAX mainframe, provides program downloads and other support functions such as program listings for a variety of process control devices. The MIDB function, running on an IBM Series 1, maintains a database for vehicle scheduling, and it gives "online" data to control devices concerning vehicle options, completion status, and paint color selection.

Figure 11.3 Direct interaction via the LAN.

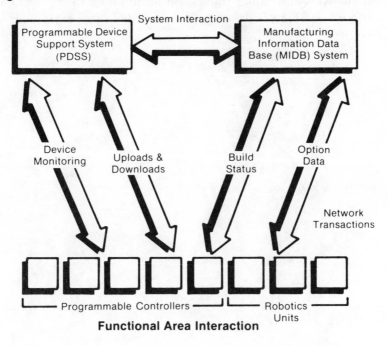

The automation control devices include programmable controllers and robot controls. The programmable controllers direct conveyors and other material handling devices that feed the body shop and paint process. The robot controls are a component of the body weld process.

LAN transactions include device monitoring, device uploads and downloads, status notification, and retrieval of vehicle option data. All these processes interact for such automated tasks as painting a car.

The vehicle's body carries identification numbers that are scanned by RF sensors connected to the programmable controllers. At several "read points," the ID numbers are then transmitted to the MIDB system, which uses them to find the vehicle's manifest. The color selection from the manifest is then sent to the programmable controllers for subsequent control of paint application.

This MIDB database connection has been proved at a major automotive facility and is under consideration for future use. The PDSS robotics LAN is already being installed in a growing number of factories.

David R. Coffin
Intel Corporation

12

Technical and Office Protocols (TOP)

Chapter 11 describes the Manufacturing Automation Protocol (MAP) effort initiated by General Motors. Today, that protocol involves over two hundred corporations. A parallel effort, sponsored by Boeing and others, aims to produce industry-wide Technical and Office Protocol (TOP) standards. The MAP and TOP groups, whose sanctioned protocols are compatible at the higher OSI layers, seek to provide a large enough uniform market so that LAN manufacturers can achieve economies of scale.

Each industry group is selecting and sanctioning particular protocols already available. Some of these are promulgated by established standards committees, such as the International Standards Organization (ISO), and the Consultative Committee on International Telegraphy and Telephony (CCITT). But not all necessary services have yet been addressed by existing official standards. Thus, in at least some cases de facto standards must be selected by the system planner.

To be of real use in promoting network compatibility, any widely used (de facto) standard must also be published so that any supplier is able to support it. Even if they serve as the basis for popular LANs, unpublished standards run the risk of being considered proprietary rather than general.

WHAT AN OFFICE LAN MUST DO

There are five broad categories which an office LAN must cover:

- Interconnect PCs and intelligent workstations for information sharing and mail or messaging.
- Enable network users to access mainframes to get at data, applications and other resources which reside only there.
- Support cooperative processing among these three classes of intelligent systems.
- Allow sharing of expensive or scarce resources and peripherals.
- Deliver all its services in a secure and administrable framework.

In terms of the OSI layers, these tasks can be recast in three main groupings of the layers: Layers 5-7, a set of applications which implement the various services delivered by the LAN; Layers 3 and 4, a message delivery system that ensures reliable end-to-end communications on the LAN; and Layers 1 and 2, a controller providing physical and logical network access to the message delivery component. See Figure 12.1.

Figure 12.1 LAN elements and the OSI model.

OSI Model	LAN Elements
Application	Service Applications
Presentation	
Session	
Transport	Message Delivery
Network	
Data Link	Network Access
Physical	

Physical Network

TEN LAN SERVICES RELATED TO TOP

There are at least ten distinct office related services that a good LAN might perform:

1. *File access.* Files and records of files are accessed via the LAN as if they were local to the requesting device. As described in Chapter 6, file access should support file and record level locking. Complete file access protocols delineate both sequential and random file sharing across the LAN. One of the de facto standards available is NFA/SMB, established jointly by Intel, IBM and Microsoft.

2. *File transfer.* Files are transferred between two separate nodes on the LAN. Comprehensive protocols should enable transfer of many file types (such as binary, ASCII and graphic) and transform among standard file types. The TOP choice of protocol is the File Transfer Access and Management (FTAM) of the International Standards Organization.

3. *File archiving.* Cross-network file backup and restore saves the cost of having a mechanism for it in every node requiring backup. If accompanied by good administrative tools, effective data management can be introduced to the usually less rigorous PC and workstation users.

4. *Messaging and mail.* Mail in an office LAN (see Chapter 9) is critical for time utility in brief communications. While users' offices may be near each other, their schedules and agendas may be quite far apart. Messaging is the underlying construct for delivering an electronic mail protocol and should be robust and reliable. The TOP choice of protocol is X.400 of CCITT.

5. *Program interface.* An office network must support process-to-process or program-to-program communication across the LAN to have cooperative processing. While applications historically were optimized for large mainframes, future applications will be optimized for distributed processing based on LAN PCs and workstations.

   The TOP choice of protocol is the Common Application Service Elements (CASE) of the International Standards Organization. APPC is an IBM variation, limited to SNA computers. The LU6.2 type of SNA entity is described in Chapter 9.

6. *Remote batch.* This service enables users and administrators to submit batch jobs for execution. It is used to schedule large tasks such as database downloads at hours that will not overload the network during peak use. There is no TOP standard as of this writing. PU 2.1 (described for SNA in Chapter 9) and NETBIOS are IBM system network interfaces, respectively for mainframes and PCs.

7. *Virtual terminal.* This service allows users to log onto other machines on the LAN as if they were directly attached. Virtual terminal services are crucial to retrofitting a LAN into an existing information system, because older applications can thus be accessed as they were designed to be accessed—from a slave terminal.

8. *Printer sharing and spooling.* Prioritization, job status checking and print filtering (assured compatibility of the application and printer) are advanced features of print services.

9. *Mainframe gateways.* Mainframe access must be available, whether based on direct support of the mainframe on the LAN or by emulation of mainframe terminal cluster controllers and terminal devices, as discussed in Chapters 8 and 9.

10. *Internetworking.* An office LAN must recognize not only peer nodes on a network but also peer networks. Users of a given site's LAN must be able transparently to access nodes in another site's (or department's) LAN. LAN services must also be available to access unlike networks' resources, as discussed in Chapters 7 and 8.

Two other services worth considering are beyond the scope of this chapter. Video transmission is touched upon in Chapter 4, and voice switching is described in Chapter 9.

SUMMARY OF TOP PROTOCOLS

The shaded portions of Figure 12.2 represent the standards sanctioned in TOP. Other popular office automation standards are also listed for comparison.

Figure 12.2 TOP standards for Figure 12.1.

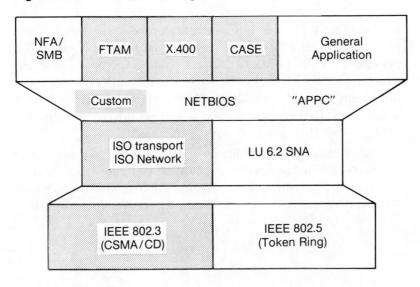

Figure 12.3 Some available office LANs.

PRODUCT	DECnet	T Ring	OpenNET	Netware
MANUFACTURER	DEC	IBM	Intel	Novell
FILE ACCESS	no	yes	yes	yes
FILE TRANSFER	yes	yes	yes	yes
FILE ARCHIVE	yes	no	yes	yes
MESSAGING/MAIL	yes	no	yes	yes
PROGRAM INTERFACE	no	yes	yes	yes
REMOTE BATCH	yes	no	yes	no
VIRTUAL TERMINAL	yes	yes	yes	no
PRINT SHARING	yes	yes	yes	yes
GATEWAYS TO HOST	yes	yes	yes	yes
INTERNETWORKING	yes	no	yes	yes

SOME COMMERCIALLY AVAILABLE LANS

Intel's OpenNET is one of the newer LAN products designed explicitly to fulfill the available TOP standards. Novell's Netware is a popular PC LAN product, usually accompanied by a file server, which uses gateways for external access. DECnet DOS, while using proprietary protocols, provides PCs with the same functions as VAXes on the LAN. IBM's Token Ring is largely proprietary but also uses the published IBM protocols noted earlier.

Figure 12.3 lists a small fraction of the LANs available and should not necessarily be assumed to contain the best one for the reader's installation. Increasingly, LAN products will be produced which meet TOP standards as well as providing the ten services discussed here.

13

Summary

CHAPTER 1—INTRODUCTION TO LOCAL AREA NETWORKS

General purpose Local Area Networks (LANs) are not restricted to a single business use or to the products of a single manufacturer. Most LANs are originally purchased to share disk storage, but other common uses are electronic mail, laser printer sharing, common access to another LAN or a mainframe computer, or joint access to public data networks and services.

In addition to being privately owned and controlled, a true LAN has equal connectivity, the ability of each station to communicate directly with every other station. Timesharing based on mainframes does not have this, since the central processing unit (CPU) must actively decide what to do with every station's output, including whether or not to send a copy to some other station.

A small LAN may sometimes be implemented by purchasing appropriate cabling, plus PC cards and/or floppy disks to run the network and properly identify its nodes.

The topology (logical shape) of a LAN can usually be described as a bus (IEEE 802.3, 802.4), ring (802.5) or star. Connections between nodes can be accomplished over twisted pair, thin coaxial cable, standard coaxial cable, or optical fiber. Respectively, these carry progressively larger flows of information (bandwidth), expressed in megabits per second (Mb/s). Connections between similar LANs are accomplished through devices called bridges; other devices, known as gateways, connect LANs to the outside world.

OPEN SYSTEMS INTERCONNECTION - OSI

LAN functionality can be described (and negotiated) in terms of seven fairly distinct layers, collectively known as the Open Systems Interconnection (OSI) model of ANSI.

Layer 7 (the Application Layer) is the only direct contact with programs or users; it includes the software interface for such functions as file transfer and security checking. Layer 6 (Presentation Layer) performs the translation function and includes terminal emulators and print or file servers. Layer 5 (Session) governs the actual startup, maintenance, and shutdown of the dialogue between two intelligent entities on the LAN.

Layer 4 (Transport) manages the actual flow of data packets (frames), while Layer 3 (Network) performs routing functions in less simple LANs or between two or more of them. Layer 2 (Data Link) assembles the actual packets and notifies Layer 4 when an error is detected in a received packet. Layer 1 (Physical) deals with cabling, signal strengths, and the decision of whether to have one channel (baseband) or many channels (broadband) on the cable or other transmission medium. This lowest layer also arbitrates among those sharing the network resource, generally through token passing or CSMA/CD ("listening").

MAP and TOP are standards being developed by GM, Boeing and other leaders in the manufacturing and office/engineering industries. These protocols specify exactly what should and should not be used to implement each of the OSI layers.

CHAPTER 2—SOME THOUGHTS ON PLANNING A LAN

A modest consulting or engineering firm probably has neither the time nor the resources to do on-site trials or even extensive visits to nearby LAN installations. They will find the advice of a trusted retail dealer worthwhile. Very large concerns (or their units) may want instead to negotiate directly with the LAN manufacturer.

Selection and implementation of a LAN involves several considerations. Where weather and throughput permit, cheaper media can be used: twisted pair instead of cable or fiber, optical LED instead of laser. Coaxial or fiber should be used in harsh environments. In any case, professionals should install the media. A network's ability to diagnose and predict its own failure should be considered. Quick repair should be facilitated by simple layouts and well-established procedures. The network should anticipate expansion. If possible, overall building design should incorporate "intelligence" along with the water pipes and heating ducts.

A 1986 American Management Association survey found that in the next year corporations planned to increase PCs by 40 percent and the networking of PCs by 100 percent. Thus the reader's planning efforts should encourage input from other departments, possibly including the pooling of resources. If not consulted, they may express offense later when the installed LAN ignores a key concern. This is important because once a LAN is ordered, new concerns and uses evolve, such as shared laser printing.

Twisted pair (telephone) cable is smaller and cheaper than coaxial cable ("coax"). But coax has either wire mesh or external metal wrapping as a shield against radio frequency interference (RFI). Shielded twisted resists external interference but does not prevent the elements of the two pair from interfering electromagnetically with each other.

Twisted pair is physically flexible. It can fit in small crevices and make sharp turns. Coax diameters range from one quarter inch up, and a coax cable requires two or more inches of radius to make a turn.

Coaxial can carry far higher frequencies than twisted pair, and thus it (or fiber) is the preferred medium for broadband. Coaxial can carry much larger data rates than twisted pair, typically ten megabits vs. one megabit.

Baseband LANs may play vanilla to broadband's tutti frutti, but where needs are more limited they are cheaper, simpler to install and easier to expand.

CHAPTER 3—A PRACTICAL LOOK AT BASEBAND

Most office LANs use baseband technology. In baseband all information is transmitted as a stream of 1's and 0's, each signal occupying the entire medium.

A LAN may have shared resources in the form of servers for files, database, directory of resources, printing, gateway and electronic mail.

Cable size affects broadband data capacity. A simple twisted pair network may only transmit one Mb/s. An Ethernet (802.3) LAN using thin coaxial (RG-58/U) can support hundreds of nodes and transmit at 10 Mb/s. The use of bridges can boost the effective data rate to many times this.

Baseband costs less than broadband, partly because modems are not needed. But broadband can carry multiple channels and is better suited to transmitting analog signals such as video.

CHAPTER 4—BROADBAND DIVERSITY AND CABLING

Broadband uses TV cable and transmission, a mature and therefore reliable technology. Video, voice and digital data can coexist on the same medium because both analog and digital transmission encoding methods are possible. Through a device called a modem, digital signals are modulated into electromagnetic waves and demodulated back to digits at the receiving end. The variety of devices that can be driven or supported includes radio, TV, telephone, computers, terminals and cameras. Equipment can be placed on any node.

A broadband LAN is flexible. Running on coaxial cable (or optical fiber), it can easily bridge or gateway to other LANs (including baseband) or to microwave or satellite transmission. It supports both token and CSMA/CD arbitration.

There can be flexible assignment of channels in both directions, and the ratio of price to data throughput (bandwidth Mb/s) is low. In fact, broadband can serve as a backbone over which many baseband LANs are carried. The number of backward channels (incoming to the headend) increases over four broad frequency spectrum classifications: low split, medium split, high split, and dual cable.

All broadband LANs run on 75 ohm coaxial cable of varying thicknesses. Three-quarter inch jacketed coax (or optical fiber) is preferable between buildings, half-inch coax for trunks within buildings, and RG-xx within business units. To minimize disturbance, LAN cable should be laid safely away from, not near, telephone system wires that may some day need fixing.

CHAPTER 5—OPTICAL FIBER: TRUTH AMID BLUE SKY

Typical fibers are thinner (3mm), lighter (55 lb/mi), more flexible and more elastic than coaxial cables. They cost about 25 cents per foot and are getting cheaper.

Optical fiber is inherently more difficult to break into undetected. Being a nonconductor it is unaffected by EMI, nor does it radiate signals that might disturb sensitive equipment nearby. There are no grounding, shock or lightning problems.

In an active optical ring, each station regenerates the signal. Optical LANs are used mostly in ring and star topologies. In a passive star network, a central star coupler divides up the incoming signal and reroutes it to each of the transceivers on the network.

The new FDDI and MAN standards involve dual counter-rotating fiber rings. The second ring runs in a paired cable, with the signal going in the opposite direction. It is entirely redundant to the first and becomes important only when a station fails or the cable is severed. Then the node nearest the break on either side "shortstops" the incoming signal and sends the outgoing signal only into the reverse direction fiber cable. Thus the two broken rings have been spliced at the breaks to form one intact ring.

CHAPTER 6—NETWORK OPERATING SYSTEMS AND SECURITY

A LAN's operating system programs manage what happens on the network. Three categories are disk service, file service and total resource service.

A LAN based on a disk server protects files only to the extent that a file's owner may prevent others from updating it. The operating system may also set aside a shared area to be controlled by application software packages, not itself.

File service LANs provide differentiated file locking for each file. After signing on with a password, the user still needs rights to access particular sets of files through such verbs as READ and DELETE. Groups of users can be given rights together, and the file owner may still set file flags to restrict access further.

File access itself consumes the great bulk of file-related transactions. Access time can be lowered by using directory hashing, directory caching, (entire) file caching, or elevator seeking.

The current crop of LANs for IBM compatible PCs are generally compatible with DOS 3.1.

CHAPTER 7—BRIDGES BETWEEN LOCAL AREA NETWORKS

A bridge copies (or reassembles) frames received from its LAN and passes them on to a compatible LAN on the other side. For continuity of service, it is best not to have one device perform both bridging and user tasks.

Bridges can overcome LAN address exhaustion, data transmission overload, overlong distances, growth constraints due to obsolete hardware, and the historical separation of two LANs that must now be joined.

The packets entering a bridge include addresses of nodes along the LANs it connects. It operates at OSI Layer 2 and/or Layer 1.

CHAPTER 8—GATEWAYS AND COMMON CARRIERS

A LAN uses a gateway to converse with WANs, mainframe computers and other LANs that have distinctly different packet protocols. Gateway servers translate one network protocol to another, overcoming both hardware and software incompatibility. While bridges ignore the higher OSI layers, gateways can translate all seven layers in the protocol if necessary.

The most popular WAN is CCITT's X.25, which in many telephone applications has replaced hard wired temporary circuits with virtual (packet) circuits between the same two points. Using a LAN-like line sharing eliminates much of the wasted idle time one would encounter on a single-conversation leased line. X.25 supports GTE Telenet, Tymnet and other public packet switching services.

IBM's System Network Architecture (SNA) is an effective way for LANs to access IBM host computers. A single SNA gateway might make a collection of PCs on an Ethernet LAN all look like 3278 terminals to the IBM mainframe.

Routers are intermediate between bridges and gateways. They do not change protocols as gateways do. But unlike bridges they do utilize OSI Layer 3. A router accepts a packet from one LAN and, by inspecting the Network Layer, decides which external LAN should receive it.

CHAPTER 9—AUTOMATED OFFICE: MAIL, FILES, VOICE, AND IMAGE

Even the simplest LANs generally provide four network-based services: print servers let the user keep working while hundreds of pages are printed silently. Electronic mail can broadcast the same memo form, personally addressed to everyone on a selected distribution list. File servers permit access to all but with varying levels of security. And gateways connect the LAN with CPUs, WANs and other outside entities.

A typical electronic mail screen provides a list of functions for selection, along with appropriate entry fields for memorandum data. A second screen displays a selection of mail available.

XMODEM, the most popular protocol for asynchronous file transmission among PCs, allows up to 128 bytes of data per packet and employs a checksum byte.

IBM's SNA networks now provide for some peer connectivity through the introduction of the PU 2.1 classification of devices. The company's DISOSS software transmits files.

PBXs are not LANs but do interface with them.

CHAPTER 10—YOU DON'T HAVE TO FIRE THE MAINFRAME

IBM's own WAN protocol (SNA) has become slightly less centralized by adding the device classification, Physical Unit type 2.1 (PU 2.1). The major mainframe still sits at the center of its world, but now certain intelligent devices are permitted to communicate directly with each other on an SNA network.

LANs allow much more connectivity than that. A LAN can support a true intermixture of three types of processing: interactive systems, background processing and specialized services. Every node, including the mainframe computer, occupies an equally endowed node along the LAN.

At the beginning of this transformation the mainframe computer sits as sole master at the center of its world as the LAN approaches with its entourage of PCs, servers and workstations. Afterward, as the LAN rides off into the sunset, the entire mainframe is hooked onto one of its nodes, being dragged along as just another peripheral device.

CHAPTER 11—MAP PROTOCOLS AND THE FACTORY

Half the cost of automating new and retooled factories may be tied to communications supporting multiple proprietary networks. In some facilities, six or more communications wiring schemes run parallel to each other.

GM founded a 21-company Manufacturing Automation Protocol (MAP) group to promote protocol and cable standardization. Two hundred corporations now participate.

Protocols of the International Standards Organization have been selected for OSI Layers 3, 4, 5 and 7. The Application Layer, for example, uses particular formats for file transfer, programming device communication and interfacing with lower layers.

IEEE 802.4 (token bus) is specified for OSI Layers 1 and 2. A broadband backbone carries many "carrier band" subnetworks for actual device nodes in the factory cells. Carrier band, although running on coax, occupies the entire branch cable for one subnetwork's binary data.

CHAPTER 12—TECHNICAL AND OFFICE PROTOCOLS (TOP)

An office LAN must interconnect PCs and intelligent workstations with mainframes, both for access of the host's programs and data and to support cooperative processing.

Several of these ten LAN services already have official standards under TOP, the Technical and Office Protocol: file access, file transfer file archiving, messaging/mail, program interface, remote batch, virtual terminal, printer sharing, mainframe gateways, and internet-working.

MAP and TOP protocols coincide at the upper Layers of OSI.

APPENDIX—QUANTITATIVE EVALUATION OF NETWORKS

Defining objectives for a network, and investigating the products available, requires two parallel efforts. A survey of relevant company personnel determines which features are important. Separately, technicians determine which functionality is present on which network product.

A preprinted Network Evaluation Form lists eighty key considerations which are translated by the preceding text into unambiguous specifications for the best LAN for that corporation. By following the accompanying instructions, network planners can construct a weighted scale by which to score the competing configurations being investigated.

Richard G. Lefkon

Appendix

Quantitative Evaluation of Networks

Defining objectives for a network, and investigating the products available, requires parallel efforts.

A technical person or team determines whether or not each LAN product investigated possesses the feature in question. Separately, a survey of relevant company personnel determines which features are very important and which are not applicable to anticipated needs.

Thus two types of data can be gathered concerning eighty common features: presence or absence of these features in each product, and numeric weightings which permit the features to be ranked as to their importance.

The Network Evaluation Form can also be used independently of the methodology discussed here.

NUMERICAL RATINGS

It is possible to weight the importance of any particular network feature on a four-point scale:

0 — not germane, even if a nice feature
1 — a desirable capability
2 — must have in final network
4 — a "drop dead" feature: must be in original LAN product.

These ratings are hard, qualitative choices to be made by each person who fills in the Network Evaluation Form:

0: *Not germane* — Diamond-studded, gold-filled cable may have some aesthetic justification for its higher cost. The ability of a word processor hookup to support teleconferencing is not needed by that business; it should not contribute to a LAN product's point score.

1: *Desirable* — This capability will probably be needed in the long run. If it does not appear in the "final" network setup at this time, it can be added later through some combination of servers, bridges and gateways.

2: *Must have* — This feature, although not required of the "off the shelf" product, is an essential capability and was instrumental in justifying the cost of the purchase.

3: (There is no "3," as explained below. If someone returns the Network Evaluation Form with 3's on it, send back a blank form and explain the instructions again.)

4: *Drop dead factor* — For smaller installations: the "vanilla" LAN product is the only purchase at this time. This capability is necessary, and several LANs do include it integrally in the "starter set" of features.

For larger installations: this necessary function is often implemented in a complex or unreliable way. The company does not plan to be a test site for new technology, and therefore the primary vendor must propose and contractually stand behind a configuration which includes this feature, even though not all products are their own.

The absence of a "3" rating has two uses: the unequal interval promotes real thinking about the choice, rather than an impressionistic checkmark along a continuous number line. Also, it sets apart the "drop dead" features so that fewer are chosen and those that are have more than twice the average weight.

COUNTING KEY BALLOTS MORE THAN ONCE ("WEIGHTING THE RATINGS")

The top of the Network Evaluation Form has a small "R.W." accompanied by a blank space. This enables the reader to obtain input from all appropriate individuals who may desire to have a say in the network they will eventually be required to use or support.

If the company has many user opinions and only one engineer, the engineer's Network Evaluation Form should be coded with a rating weight (R.W.) factor of ten or more, so that legitimate user desires do not numerically overwhelm the single known source of technical expertise. In other instances, implicit concurrence of many minor players may also be desired. In such cases, the "R.W." blanks of those with a greater say should be made higher than 1; and the most critical forms receive even higher weighting.

It is of great importance that the "R.W." blank be filled in at the time the respondent's name is entered on the Network Evaluation Form prior to distribution. This keeps the tally honest and prevents post hoc downgrading of unwelcome concerns that are nonetheless important.

The reader may observe that drop dead factors receive a quantitative rating that can be averaged with other ratings of the same LAN functionality. A drop dead factor on a small network may possibly be accommodated by purchasing a less expensive LAN and a proven enhancement, for lower overall cost. In large installations, mutually exclusive capabilities may be perceived to be in this category, and it is useful to be able to rank among them. Whenever somebody's drop dead factor is downgraded, some effort should be made to explain the reasons why it makes sense to do so.

CUSTOMIZING RESPONSES

Anecdotal input is facilitated by the Network Evaluation Form. If the form is photocopied (or retyped—see next and last paragraphs) on one side of the paper, a full page on the reverse side is made available for free form descriptive responses. These may include special requests, suggested vendors or site visitations, or the detailed recounting of good or bad network experiences for consideration by the network planner.

The Network Evaluation Form does not have explicit instructions on its face concerning anecdotal input. This is because some readers will want respondents to restrict themselves to quantitative surveys only.

Special care should be taken in the distribution of complete instructions on how to use the Network Evaluation Form. These should take the form of individually addressed, individually typed, signed letters. The cover letters should contain a true sending date and should also contain a reasonably firm cutoff date. The reply date (at least ten days out) should be stated courteously but clearly, so that recipients know it is their own free choice if they do not respond.

TALLYING THE RESPONSES ("RATING THE WEIGHTINGS")

Once the forms are returned, a tally sheet like the one in Figure A.1 should be prepared. On it are written every name, the corresponding "R.W.," and the number answered to each question (in alternate boxes) for that person. This puts all the numbers in one place and allows the raw data forms to be archived.

Depending on the number of forms returned, a pencil or hand held calculator or PC program can be used to multiply each individual question response (Q's) by the "R.W." for that respondent. For instance, the result of each calculation Q1 * R.W. is placed in W1, the weighted point total for Question 1 for that respondent.

Finally, all W1's from all respondents are totaled, divided by the Total Weight, and placed in RW1, the relative weight of LAN Feature #1.

Figure A.1 Tally form for network evaluation form.

NAME	R.W.	Q1 W1	Q2 W2	Q3 W3	Q4 W4	etc.
_____	___	__ ___	__ ___	__ ___	__ ___	__ __
_____	___	__ ___	__ ___	__ ___	__ ___	__ __
_____	___	__ ___	__ ___	__ ___	__ ___	__ __
_____	___	__ ___	__ ___	__ ___	__ ___	__ __
etc.	etc.	etc.				

TOTAL WEIGHT_____ RW1: RW2: RW3: RW4: RW5:

Top Score: _____ _____ _____ _____ _____

$$\overline{(RW1 + RW2 + \text{etc.})}$$

The process just described will produce relative ratings of approximately one to two points per feature, with each functionality having a maximum possible point rating of 4 and a minimum possible rating of zero.

If 1.25 is the average of the final weightings, then the theoretical top score on 80 questions will be 100. The actual TOP SCORE may be 75 or it may be 125, but it will be large enough to separate the competing LAN products into clear groupings. Selection of a LAN from the top grouping can then be made on the basis of price considerations and other factors.

SAME FORMS FOR YES/NO TECHNICAL DATA ("RATING")

Now the organized LAN investigation begins. It may start or conclude with a formal request for proposal (RFP), or it can occur in any of several other ways. Information and methods contained in earlier chapters of this book will probably be useful along the way.

The Network Evaluation Form can simplify the task if reused to track the features of each competing LAN or configuration. Here the vendor contact and location are entered in the "user name" area and the person assigned to that investigation fills in the "return to" spaces. For each of the fifty features, a "Y" or "N" is entered (in the "importance" column) without regard to the relative rating given to that particular LAN feature. This helps in two ways: first, as business needs evolve, more features may be needed and the cost of much further investigation will be avoided. Second, the LAN investigation can be performed independently of, perhaps simultaneously with, the user survey.

The Tally Form can similarly be reused to summarize the results of the investigation and facilitate the final evaluation and choice. Here again, the vendor name is used in place of an individual respondent's name. But the top blank line is marked "WEIGHTING" and on it are entered the overall question ratings gotten from the user survey effort. This information may come in before or after the Y/N technical specifications are obtained, but these importance ratings must still go on the top line.

As the technical Y/N evaluations of each LAN are completed, the Y's and N's are written in the Q1, Q2, Q3, etc., columns of the line where that vendor's name has been written. This information can be entered even before the results of the user survey are known.

Once both the survey phase and the technical evaluation phase have been completed, the master Tally Form will contain three types of information. "WEIGHTING" and the name of each vendor will appear in the first ("NAME") column. The point value of each question will appear in the W1, W2, etc., columns of the top line, which has already been labeled "WEIGHTING." And for every other line, there will be eighty Y's and N's in the Q columns corresponding to the presence or absence of that feature in the product that has been evaluated.

From this point, assigning a total numeric score to each vendor is extremely simple. Features which are present will add that weighting factor to a LAN's score; features that are absent won't. Thus, wherever an N appears in a Q column on that line, write a zero in the corresponding W column immediately to the right. Wherever a Y appears in a Q column for that vendor, copy the WEIGHTING factor for that question from the top line into the W column immediately to the right of the Y. Once this is done for each vendor line, sum that line and place the total in the R.W. column immediately to the right of that vendor's name.

The resulting Tally Form contains a viable number rating adjacent to the name of each vendor. Experience has shown that these overall vendor scores fall into fairly neat groupings and narrow the choices to a manageable number. Including this final Tally Form as an appendix to the LAN budget proposal keeps higher management well-informed about the choices investigated and the reasons for the present recommendation.

FOLLOW-UP CONTACTS ("WAITING")

While the user community is awaiting the outcome, certain contacts will of course be helpful. As soon as the relative weightings of the eighty LAN capabilities have been computed, it is a good idea to distribute them to higher management as well as to all participants in the survey. The top of the organization will know that progress is being made, and in what direction; and those surveyed will appreciate knowing how their peers responded, even though the overall results will not concur with their own in every category.

The contact information on the Network Evaluation Form can be extremely useful in doing follow-up, especially on anecdotal information. Also, technicians or users can be contacted more easily for advice relating to the business uses of the network.

COPYRIGHT PROTECTION

The Network Evaluation Form is an integral part of an American Management Association book, the Management Briefing entitled *Selecting a Local Area Network*. It may be photocopied or retyped in entirety for local use by an owner of this book. Public reproduction without written permission is expressly forbidden.

Also excluded is elimination of any information on the form during duplication. A subsequent book or article may appear based on experiences related by persons and corporations using this form in selecting a local area network. Therefore it is necessary to preserve the contact information therein. The reader's cooperation is appreciated.

NETWORK EVALUATION FORM

Network Evaluation Form   *R.W.* ____   *Please Return To:*

Name: _____   (further info on   _____
                        using form is
Location: _____   available: AMA   _____
_____   LAN BOOK   _____
Telephone: ( )   c/o D. Lefkon   ( )
                        609 West 114 St.
                        NYC, NY 10025
                        212-663-2315)

Instructions: *Categories:*

Please mark each question to indicate the   0: Not Germane
importance of that network function in   1: Desirable
helping you do your job better.   2: Necessary
                                                   4: A "drop dead"
Your eighty responses can probably be   factor
made in less than five minutes. Please
answer each with a 0, 1, 2 or 4.

Question   *Importance*

If we install a network, should it . . .
Questions follow

GENERAL PRACTICES

Q1:   Be used by other departments (if answer is
      not 0, please list):
      _____ _____ _____?   0   1   2   3   4
Q2:   Permit video transmission (such as CATV
      or teleconferencing)?   0   1   2   3   4
Q3:   Explicitly permit hookup to local cable
      television?   0   1   2   3   4

Selecting a Local Area Network—113

Q4:	Provide for voice transmission (in-house or externally)?	0	1	2	3	4
Q5:	Explicitly provide for using telephone company lines?	0	1	2	3	4
Q6:	Handle the sending and receiving of very large data files?	0	1	2	3	4
Q7:	Deliver thousands of small messages per second between stations?	0	1	2	3	4
Q8:	Supply an electronic mail facility between stations?	0	1	2	3	4
Q9:	Have one or more central printers (e.g., laser)?	0	1	2	3	4
Q10:	Let a central disk drive impersonate individual PC disks?	0	1	2	3	4
Q11:	Support "background" processing sent by workstations?	0	1	2	3	4
Q12:	Serve also as a conduit for "centralized" CPU timesharing?	0	1	2	3	4
Q13:	Have uncomplicated and effective user instructions?	0	1	2	3	4
Q14:	Provide menus and help screens?	0	1	2	3	4
Q15:	Supply each user online instructions on each device?	0	1	2	3	4
Q16:	Have clear and extensive network management documentation?	0	1	2	3	4
Q17:	Provide a help phone for the network administrator?	0	1	2	3	4

PLANNING NETWORK SIZE

Q18:	Be small and simple enough to buy from a retail dealer?	0	1	2	3	4
Q19:	Be extensive enough to justify labor for on-site trials?	0	1	2	3	4
Q20:	Eventually connect no more than 35 users?	0	1	2	3	4
Q21:	Eventually connect between 35 and 200 users?	0	1	2	3	4

Q22: Connect nearly a thousand users, or more?   0   1   2   3   4

Q23: Have a total cable path length of at least a mile?   0   1   2   3   4

Q24: Connect more than one floor?   0   1   2   3   4

Q25: Connect more than one building per location?   0   1   2   3   4

Q26: Connect more than one geographical area?   0   1   2   3   4

Q27: Choose among alternate signal routes for quicker delivery?   0   1   2   3   4

Q28: Forbid any station from sending a second block of data until all the others have had a chance to send?   0   1   2   3   4

Q29: Let the stations with the most to say send the most?   0   1   2   3   4

Q30: Provide the facility to connect many thousands of devices?   0   1   2   3   4

Q31: Facilitate expansion later on without extensive changes?   0   1   2   3   4

Q32: Facilitate rearrangement of itself without major recabling?   0   1   2   3   4

Q33: Initially include the outlay for central "patch panels"?   0   1   2   3   4

Q34: Be able to survive a misguided first-time layout?   0   1   2   3   4

CABLING AND HARDWARE

Q35: Avoid having to cable each station directly to a central point?   0   1   2   3   4

Q36: Run through harsh environments or underground?   0   1   2   3   4

Q37: Withstand interference from nearby transmitters or machines?   0   1   2   3   4

Q38: Have wiring that absolutely will fit in small crevices?   0   1   2   3   4

Q39: Use lines that can make sharp right-angle turns?   0   1   2   3   4

Q40: Use exclusively indoor cabling?	0	1	2	3	4
Q41: Use cabling that conforms to strict local fire laws?	0	1	2	3	4
Q42: Have high resistance to rodents and other small animals?	0	1	2	3	4
Q43: Maintain a very high signal-to-noise ratio?	0	1	2	3	4
Q44: Function where sparks or shocks can be deadly?	0	1	2	3	4
Q45: Run many distinct subnetworks (channels) on one cable?	0	1	2	3	4
Q46: If a "broadcast" medium, have mostly outgoing channels?	0	1	2	3	4
Q47: If "broadcast," have roughly equal incoming and outgoing channels?	0	1	2	3	4
Q48: Define very many clearly delimited channels?	0	1	2	3	4
Q49: Resist unauthorized tapping of the signal?	0	1	2	3	4
Q50: Support workstations that are not IBM compatible (please list): _____ _____ _____?	0	1	2	3	4

SECURITY AND AVAILABILITY

Q51: Be nearly impossible to tap undetected?	0	1	2	3	4
Q52: Keep functioning smoothly even if the cable is severed in two?	0	1	2	3	4
Q53: Automatically remove a disabled station from the network?	0	1	2	3	4
Q54: Keep running even if one fifth of the stations fail?	0	1	2	3	4
Q55: Perform invisible re-tries for reconnection if the circuit fails?	0	1	2	3	4
Q56: Assign "permanent" unique names to workstations and server units?	0	1	2	3	4
Q57: Let users place passwords on their own files?	0	1	2	3	4

Q58: Protect some files so that only the owner can change them? 0 1 2 3 4

Q59: Assign users READ, DELETE, etc. abilities for each file? 0 1 2 3 4

Q60: Be able to assign these access rights to groups of users? 0 1 2 3 4

Q61: Let each file's owner restrict this assignment? 0 1 2 3 4

Q62: Provide "uncontrolled shared" areas for software package data? 0 1 2 3 4

Q63: Protect access to every resource, not just files? 0 1 2 3 4

Q64: Have modifiable software as its (network's) basis? 0 1 2 3 4

Q65: Be installed exclusively as VLSI insert boards? 0 1 2 3 4

Q66: Produce formatted reports on its (network's) health and status? 0 1 2 3 4

Q67: Enable online probing of its (network's) health and status? 0 1 2 3 4

FILES AND EXTERNAL ACCESS

Q68: Phrase its file commands in unaltered PC language? 0 1 2 3 4

Q69: Facilitate fast-core storage of pointers to files and records? 0 1 2 3 4

Q70: Support storing an entire file in fast core? 0 1 2 3 4

Q71: Provide file servers which optimize (resequence) requests? 0 1 2 3 4

Q72: Support not just files but a centralized formal database? 0 1 2 3 4

Q73: Augment another network already in use? 0 1 2 3 4

Q74: Interact with "identical" other networks? 0 1 2 3 4

Q75: Join with another network of different data rate? 0 1 2 3 4

Q76: Communicate with an X.25 Wide Area
Network?   0   1   2   3   4
Q77: Communicate with certain wide area net-
works (please list):
_____ _____ _____?   0   1   2   3   4
Q78: Explicitly assist retrieval of data from these
services:
_____ _____ _____?   0   1   2   3   4
Q79: Communicate directly with mainframe
computers made by:
_____ _____ _____?   0   1   2   3   4
Q80: Coordinate these unusual specialized processes or machines:
_____ _____ _____?   0   1   2   3   4

Authors' Directory

John Adams
Digital Equipment Corp.
P.O. Box 1123
Littleton, MA 01460-1123
617-486-7990

Albert D. Bender
FiberCom, Inc.
P.O. Box 11966
Roanoke, VA 24044-1966
703-342-6700

William Berkman
Orchid Technologies
47790 Westinghouse Drive
Freemont, CA 94539
415-490-8586

Peter Buttros
Corvus Systems, Inc.
350 Lakeside Boulevard
Hopatcong, NJ 07643
201-398-3413

David R. Coffin
Intel Corporation
2402 West Beardsley Road
Phoenix, AZ 65027
602-869-4795

Donald R. DiBrita
Nestar Systems, Inc.
420 Lexington Avenue
New York, NY 10070
212-867-2400

Efrem Goldberg
Bridge Communications, Inc.
303 Wyman Street
Waltham, MA 02154
617-890-6122

Carolyn Guzy
Bridge Communications, Inc.
303 Wyman Street
Waltham, MA 02154
617-890-6122

Kevin Hughes
Allen-Bradley
555 Briarwood Circle
Ann Arbor, MI 48104
313-668-2500

Alan W. Laster
Citibank, N.A.
111 Wall Street
New York, NY 10043
212-558-5429

Richard G. Lefkon
Citibank, N.A., and
New York University
609 West 114th Street
New York, NY 10025
212-663-2315

Charles J. Letizia
Wang Laboratories, Inc.
780 Third Avenue
New York, NY 10017
212-418-1000

Oleh Maczaj
Citibank, N.A.
111 Wall Street
New York, NY 10043
212-558-0967

Kathryn A. Petry
3Com Corp.
1365 Shorebird Way
Mountain View, CA 94039
415-961-9602

Bruce D. Schatzman
Xerox Corporation
475 Oakmead Parkway
Sunnyvale, CA 94086
408-737-4653

Cheryl Snapp
Novell, Inc.
1170 North Industrial Park Drive
Orem, UT 24054
801-226-8202

Lance S. Sprung
Wang Laboratories, Inc.
780 Third Avenue
New York, NY 10017
212-418-1000

Pamela E. Valentine
3Com Corp.
1365 Shorebird Way
Mountain View, CA 94039
415-961-9602